Divorce and the Christian:
What the Bible Teaches

Divorce & the Christian
What the Bible Teaches

Robert J. Plekker

Tyndale House
Publishers, Inc.
Wheaton, Illinois

ACKNOWLEDGMENTS

I wish to thank all those who helped me during the
writing of this book and especially those theologians
who pored over every Bible text to make sure its
application was correct.

Quotations from Scripture, unless otherwise identified,
are taken from the *New International Version.*

To my wife
JANE
with whom, after nearly thirty
years of marriage, I have a love
that grows deeper each year.
We recognize our love as a blessing
from the Originator of marriage—
our Lord—who is *Love.*

CONTENTS

FOREWORD

Divorce is rampant in our generation. Current statistics indicate that 40 percent of all marriages will end in divorce.

Now, Christian divorce does not equal the national average. Yet the fact is that divorce is quite common among evangelicals. And it is likely to get worse. More and more, divorce is looked upon as an easy out for a marital tangle. Such quarrels often have their roots in marital infidelity, at a time when marital fidelity is considered an outmoded custom.

Robert Plekker, in this book *Divorce and the Christian*, assumes that the Bible is normative and its principles are still binding upon Christian conscience. He examines the divorce problem from every perspective, including divorce between Christian and non-Christian. He discusses the vexing question of remarriage and when it is legitimate.

Particularly pertinent is the author's assertion that apart from unfaithfulness as a ground for divorce, all other reasons for breaking apart a marriage constitute a denial of Christ's Lordship.

And Dr. Plekker shows us the grace of God in such

cases, the basis for solving the tough conflicts of marriage, and the basis for forgiveness.

Divorce and the Christian may not be popular with some people. It offers no easy answers. I commend the author for tackling a difficult subject and rigorously applying God's Word to it with faithfulness and compassion.

Harold Lindsell, editor emeritus
Christianity Today, *1979*

INTRODUCTION

These days nearly everything is increasing: the price of gasoline, the cost of living, the crime rate, alcoholism, and, yes, even the number of divorces. The solutions to most of these trends are controversial, complex, and culturally variable. But within this matter of divorce, there is a specific, *unchanging* answer that requires urgent action.

Yet perhaps the most alarming escalation is divorce between Christians. Today there is hardly a church-attending family that, directly or indirectly, doesn't know the pain of divorce. As Christians, we accept announcements of divorce quietly, and we neglect to ask those persons involved if they have truly searched the Scriptures in the matter. Maybe this is because we Christians acquiesce to the forces of social change and think that the Christian view of divorce is unsubstantial in a modern world.

Another reason why we allow some of these divorce announcements to whiz by us is that to speak up carries with it a responsibility. Talking to a friend about a potential divorce or a pending one raises awkward questions. Is there such a thing as a Christian divorce? Is there a biblical precedent? Is there anything wrong in remarriage? What is the role of a friend (a third party) in a couple's process of divorce? What is the role of the Church? Is a person who remarries guilty of *continuous* adultery? How should the victim of a divorce handle the tension between his conscience and the ugly facts of life? What are the effects of divorce on the rest of the Christian community, the church, the home, and children? And too, isn't the tragedy of a marriage without love a worse thing than the pain of divorce?

These are the questions I will try to answer. My source is holy Scripture. I believe that God's Word is infallible, authoritative, credible, and as instructive in our time as it was the day it was written. Because God's Word is unchangeable, it applies to us in the same way that changed lives thousands of years ago. Indeed, the Bible is as relevant today as it ever was. Social change has not rendered the Bible obsolete.

Because Christendom seems to be swayed by the popular demand for church-approved divorce, this book comes with the prayer that God will use it to renew the holiness of the marriage bond and to establish concretely the uncompromising words of Jesus Christ on marriage, divorce, and remarriage.

ONE
Pieces of a Puzzle

Here is a paradox you see all the time: One young couple, healthy and wealthy, comes from strong Christian families and attends a Bible-believing church. Something happens in the marriage, and they get a divorce. It is sad and painful. Each party remains unhappy and restless.

But another couple in the same church has a different tragedy. The husband is permanently disabled, and the couple is poor. The wife must provide her husband twenty-four-hour care. There are frustrations and disappointments, sure, but an amazing thing happens—the second couple's love deepens and grows.

What do we see? Divorce, in the first case, and its opposite, in the second. The first couple seemed to bring divorce upon themselves. Everything was going their way, but something changed *in them.* The second couple grew a glorious love, although the circumstances were ripe for divorce. What a beautiful and inspiring image of marital dedication!

Why such a difference between the two couples? We can only surmise. Perhaps in the first couple both parties contributed to the disintegration of the marriage, while in the second couple the cause of illness was no one's fault and served as a common enemy. Perhaps hardship unites and affluence separates. We don't know. It is indeed part of a puzzle. Marriage is an inscrutable mystery. We don't always understand why love in one marriage seems different from love in another marriage.

The Symptom of Divorce

But we do know one thing. Divorce is *not* the problem. Divorce is not the problem among Christians, not in America, not even within the Church. Even Jesus Christ never labeled divorce as the problem of so many marriages. Rather, he identified divorce as a *symptom* of a deeper plight.

We can use this same illustration. Just as the problem of the disabled husband was not that he couldn't work for a living or get out of bed—those were just effects or symptoms of a more chronic problem—so the divorce of the first couple is not the problem, but a symptom of a more chronic illness.

Spiritual health is the solution to the real problem, of which divorce is a symptom, even though it is hard to recognize in the face of flying pots and pans. God's Word tells us why the spiritual problem—the chronic disease that eats away at marriage—is hard to spot. God says, "The sinful nature desires what is contrary to the Spirit, and the Spirit what is contrary to the sinful nature" (Galatians 5:17). Indeed, there is a war going on inside us.

Let's look at the reason Moses permitted divorce among the Israelites. According to Jesus, it was because their "hearts were hard" (Matthew 19:8). Today we have the Holy Spirit for this old spiritual illness. God renews the believer's heart through the Holy Spirit's indwelling. When a disease is prevented, its symptoms never appear. When the spiritual sickness of hardened hearts (the problem) is prevented by the constant presence of the Holy Spirit, the symptom of divorce cannot turn up.

Divorce is a symptom of spiritual sickness; therefore, the cure for divorce is a spiritual renewal.

Now, there are some people who would like to treat the symptom and not the problem. Some Christians would like to pretend divorce does not exist or could not possibly happen to them. By ignoring it, they also ignore the problem, which festers and grows more serious with time. And some non-Christians would like to eliminate divorce by eliminating marriage. "You can lower the divorce rate," they say, "if you alter your moral hang-ups about sex." These people advocate open marriage as a solution. But they, too, are only treating the symptom of divorce and not the problem of the spirit.

So let's not kid ourselves. Divorce is not the problem. The hardened heart is the problem and can only be cured through a deepened faith in Jesus Christ.

The Interpretation of Scripture
A friend once told me, "You can interpret the Bible in a million different ways. What one person reads and understands Scripture to say may not be the same as the next person's interpretation of the same text." Here lies another part of the puzzle. Within the situation of divorce the Bible is essential; it helps ward off the onrush of the infecting disease. Yet not all of us are in perfect exegetical harmony; that is, not everyone understands the Bible to say exactly the same things.

At first, my friend's statement bothered me because I wasn't sure whether it represented a question of interpretation or a challenge to the inspiration of holy Scripture. To clarify the point, I asked my divorced friend to give me more than one explanation of Christ's words, "What God has joined together, let man not separate," since this text (Matthew 19:6) addresses the subject at hand.

"That's a good text to use," she said, "That's exactly

the one everybody interprets differently. First my father tried to tell me that the word 'man' meant my friends who were encouraging me to get the divorce. Then my brother insisted that 'man' meant the judge in the courtroom, and my sister thought that 'man' meant my 'ex' who, in both of our opinions, had put our marriage on the rocks long before the divorce was final. So you see, right there are three different ways to read the same verse. I told you that you can interpret the Bible in many different ways!"

None of those interpretations is a good exegesis of Matthew 19:6. Nor are any a valid accusation against the clear intent of the passage. Rather, it is a classic illustration of using the Bible to justify one's position. It is an attempt to escape the force of Jesus' insistence on the permanency of marriage.

"What God hath joined together, let man not separate," contrasts what God can do as opposed to what humans may not do. Its message is clear. We may not disjoin what God has joined for life. The emphasis is not on this person or that person; it is on the contrast between God's sovereign authority and man's natural inclination to oppose him. There are not three different meanings in the words of Matthew 19:6. Instead, this verse gives us one command: Do not divorce.

Not only is an unbiased rendering of Scripture hard to come by when we are influenced by bad advice, but also when portions of the Bible seem to us insensible and unfair.

A retired pastor once confessed to me that he had a problem when the Apostle Paul expressed a delight in being single and advised some not to marry. He claimed that Paul prejudiced himself against marriage.

But one wonders if this pastor intended to toss out whole parts of Scripture just because he disagreed with Paul's feelings toward marriage. If he did that, he would have to chuck some other very important sections of the

Bible as well. For instance, after our Lord finished answering the Pharisees in Matthew 19:3–9, his disciples said to him, "If this is the situation between a husband and wife, it is better not to marry" (19:10). Jesus answered them by saying, "Some have renounced marriage because of the kingdom of heaven. The one who can accept this should accept it" (19:12b). We can conclude that Paul was only echoing what Christ had already said. So it is never wise to attack one writer of the Scripture, since we know that all Scripture supports itself throughout. Such an attack is bound to end in contradiction and failure.

But when it comes to the matter of divorce, an unprejudiced view of the Bible is most difficult, especially if the interpreter is the one involved with the divorce.

There are two options in applying Scripture to the issue of divorce. One is to treat the Bible with an open mind. The other is to recognize that divorce is an extremely personal, traumatic thing that is difficult to comprehend secondhand. The people involved have feelings which must be taken into account. But this does not mean that Scripture may be watered down in order to justify opinions or placate people. To the contrary, we are called to hold forth an uncompromised exegesis of Scripture as it *applies* to the subjective situation of a divorce.

Now, it seems to me that this can best be accomplished through those who have not been wounded by the trauma of a marital distress.

One divorcee, upon learning that I was writing this book, said to me, "How can you write a book on marriage, divorce, and remarriage if you haven't gone through a divorce yourself?" My answer was that if I had gone through a divorce myself, I would have become unavoidably prejudiced in my approach toward Scripture. One must, while studying God's Word, be willing to accept whatever he says, regardless of any personal circumstances or possible consequences. This is very difficult for any Christian directly involved. Most will admit they are trying to justify themselves by trying to fit Scripture into their case.

Finally, there are some to whom the Bible doesn't matter at all. It holds no sway over their lives. These people, when they suffer from marital bankruptcy, seek solutions from the world. They don't refer to the Bible even when the chips are down. This tells us something about the real problem behind the symptom. Some Christians allow their marital relationship to deteriorate so far that they refer to Scripture just to make themselves look good in front of other Christians who know divorce to be a sin. Still others seem convinced that they can have it both ways; that is, they are certain that they may violate the institution of marriage any number of times in the world's divorce courts and just as many times be forgiven by a loving and understanding God. But one may not continue to marry, divorce, and remarry for just any reason. One cannot be forgiven without repentance. Part of repentance is forsaking the sin!

Because some have refused to read God's Word as "Thus saith the Lord," they have often chosen a course of action that places them on a collision path with God himself. Christians actually know better, but when proliferating circumstances develop into full-blown marital crises, they are caught up in confusion and misery instead of the Holy Spirit's work through the Word.

Picking up the Pieces
When we note, therefore, the increasing rate of divorce within the Church, we measure the degree to which many Christians have ignored Christ and have temporarily hardened their hearts to his teachings on marriage and divorce. We measure, then, the severity of the symp-

tom *and* the existence of an underlying and more basic spiritual disease.

This is why an open, faithful, sensible view of the Word of God is so essential. In Scripture is found the Mystery of mysteries, the One who can help us experience the inscrutable mystery of love and marriage. The Bible is the cure, the antidote to the ravages of divorce.

But unfortunately by the time the symptom of divorce surfaces, a couple's receptivity to the Word of God is diminished. Hearts have already hardened. What one remembers of past teaching is misused, confused, or misapplied. And sometimes, as we have seen, Scripture is bent to say something that in fact it does not say.

Only through the Holy Spirit does one obtain the courage to return to Scripture honestly, to discover how Christ did away with Old Testament divorce, and how he appropriated God's softening agent for hardened hearts.

TWO
Christ Changes the Ground Rules

Marriage was instituted by God in the very beginning. God ordained marriage in the Garden of Eden before the fall of man. The consequences of the fall—sin and hardened hearts—are unavoidably linked to the real spiritual problem surrounding divorce.

Old Testament history teaches that alienation from God—the consequence of sin that hardens man's heart—is the one factor distorting marriage and sex today. It gives rise to fornication, incest, homosexuality, and adultery. None of this was present in Eden before the fall. Perhaps this is one of the reasons our Lord asks us to think about creation when we consider the subject of marriage and divorce (Matthew 19:4, 8).

Marital bliss is emotional, physical, and spiritual harmony. It is hardly the result of good fortune, or computerized matchmaking, or even ecstatic sex. You don't achieve a happy marriage by attending marriage courses or reading books about sexual technique. Marriage is a union of the spirit. Therefore, the only lasting solution for today's Christian seeking a solution to the divorce syndrome is the force present in Jesus Christ. It is Jesus who reinstituted marriage for us by reframing it within its proper perspectives. He provided all New Testament believers with divine ability to make their marriages work.

Old Testament Divorce

Old Testament believers had God's example to follow as he poured out his grace to them day by day. God used his relationship with his people as a prototype of marriage. He gave them himself as a model husband. But, true to the distorted nature of man, most Old Testament believers had a difficult time recognizing God's purpose for marriage and the family structure.

We see the Old Testament assessment of divorce in Deuteronomy 24:1: "If a man marries a woman who becomes displeasing to him because he finds something indecent about her, and he writes her a certificate of divorce, gives it to her and sends her from his house . . ." From this text, found with many other miscellaneous ordinances, we see that many Old Testament families had a bad time with marriages even back then on the vast plains of Moab. Each generation that followed made its own marital mistakes until God finally used the prophet Hosea to visually and figuratively demonstrate what marriage and reconciliation really meant.

During Moses' day, women held a subordinate position to men, and marriage was considered more of a business deal than a divinely ordained institution. The wife was actually her husband's property. He had to write her a certificate of divorce and give it to her before he could send her from his house.

The New Testament: Christ on Divorce

Old Testament grounds for divorce included just about anything one could think of—except adultery! Adultery was worse—cause for capital punishment. Christ's statements on marriage changed the entire Old Testament concept of divorce. Jesus obliterated all man-made excuses for divorce with just one statement (Matthew 19:8, 9). He insisted that our Father's original indissoluble design for marriage, as established in the Garden, had total precedence over any and all of the Mosaic allowances that the Pharisees questioned. So it wasn't until Christ's day that this matter of divorce was finally straightened out. From the beginning, God fully intended married couples to stay together until death (Genesis 2:18, 23, 24).

God's ordained unity between husband and wife has been increasingly ignored since the fall of man. God's original intent for marriage had already become so distorted by Christ's day that the Pharisees had the audacity to ask him: "Is it lawful for a man to divorce his wife for any and every reason?" (Matthew 19:3).

Isn't it interesting? The Pharisees were more concerned to know the proper way to divorce someone than how to remain happily married. Jesus' answer established the New Testament position on marriage and it surprised them.

Isn't it also striking that Jesus answers a question that had plagued mankind for generations since the fall? His answers are recorded in the Bible so that they will profit and instruct us as well; yet some of us continue to ask the same old question, "Is it lawful for a man to divorce his wife for any and every reason?" What we mean is something such as, "Can't *I* get a divorce because of *my* special reasons or unique set of circumstances?" Jesus' answer would be the same today: "Haven't you read [the Scriptures]?"

In Jesus' day there were two schools of thought on divorce, the school of Hillel and that of Shammai. They held different views on the *scope* of fornication *(porneia).* The former was conservative while the latter was more liberal. The Pharisees were testing Jesus to see whose side he would take. But instead of recognizing either alternative on divorce, Jesus went back to God's original design for marriage, saying in effect that God never intended any divorce for any reason for anyone.

But let's place ourselves in the framework of the Pharisees for just a moment. They had been deeply involved in all the rules and regulations regarding marriage and divorce for centuries, and now they were told that what God joined man could not disjoin. Consider how they must have figured that they had Jesus "nailed" now. Moses had said, "If a man marries a woman who becomes displeasing to him . . . and he writes her a certificate of divorce . . ." (Deuteronomy 24:1). So, they questioned him further about this law of Moses in an effort to trap him. " 'Why then,' they asked, 'did Moses command that a man give his wife a certificate of divorce and send her away?' " (Matthew 19:7). "Jesus replied, 'Moses permitted you to divorce your wives because your hearts were hard. But it was not this way from the beginning' " (Matthew 19:8). This was no compliment to those people in the Old Testament or to the Pharisees!

Our Lord's statement accomplished two things: Not only did Jesus reestablish God's original intent and purpose for marriage, but he also provided a solution to the problem of hardness of heart by coming to earth. In one stroke he canceled out all the cheap excuses for divorce that were, and still are, offered from man's stony heart. "I tell you that anyone who divorces his wife, except for marital unfaithfulness, and marries another woman commits adultery" (Matthew 19:9).

Without compromise, Christ set the New Testament record straight on marriage and divorce. Our Lord reemphasized that divorce is not God's way. Therefore, if a believer exercises his own will over God's will by obtaining a civil divorce through the courts of the land he isn't really divorced in God's sight.

Jesus said, "Anyone who divorces his wife, except for

24

marital unfaithfulness, and marries another woman commits adultery." Why? Why would he be committing adultery? There is only one explanation: Because he is *still married* to his first wife in God's sight.

This is true for the *woman* involved just as well. We read in Matthew 5:32 that "anyone who marries a woman so divorced commits adultery." Why? Why would a third party (removed from the whole ordeal of the divorce) be guilty of adultery? Because in God's sight the wife is still married to her husband (the one who supposedly thought he was putting her away).

The point our Lord makes here is that anyone who thinks he is divorced for reasons other than marital unfaithfulness (fornication) isn't actually divorced at all. Consequently, whoever marries a person so divorced will find he or she is not single but still married. Even the third party mentioned in Matthew 5:32 would be committing adultery.

Still, divorce happens—even among Christians. Divorce has become one of the major expressions of our sinful condition. Because this is true, it becomes incumbent on each of us to *know* the early warning signs of this fatal symptom. Marital suicide usually begins with an unharnessed self-will. Wanting our own way, in and of itself, isn't always bad. However, if our will is found to be out of harmony with God's will and we persist in it, then the evil seed of sin takes hold and grows uncontrollably. But if we obediently and immediately submit to his will at the expense of our own, the seed withers and dies. When we argue with God by rationalizing and feeding our own wills over his, we grieve his Holy Spirit and cultivate the seed of self-will, which blooms the weed of a full-blown spiritual rebellion. This leads to the hardening of one's heart—and in this case, spiritual as well as marital suicide.

Jesus Christ, on the other hand, is the effective and proven weed-killer for every evil seed in man's heart.

Therefore, a *chronic* hardening of the Christian's heart is virtually an impossibility with the indwelling of, and the surrender to, Jesus and his Holy Spirit.

So the basic difference between Old Testament and New Testament divorce lies in the person and power of Jesus Christ. If Christians would only apply this truth, they would become more keenly aware of the fact that divorce is not an option for them. The reader may ask, "Do you really mean that?" Yes, I do! When Jesus is Lord, then our excuses for hardening the heart are gone. Every need to seek a divorce is likewise swept away. God said, "I hate divorce" (Malachi 2:16). He hates it because he has fashioned marriage to be an indissoluble union between one man and one woman—for life. It's still that way today, even after the fall. God hasn't changed because of the fall—*we* have!

God created the heavens and the earth, and "God saw that it was good" (Genesis 1:10). He made man and gave him woman, and said, "For this reason a man will leave his father and mother and be united to his wife, and they shall become one flesh" (Genesis 2:24). But then man fell and destroyed his perfect state. Man also destroyed his ability to keep God's law perfectly. He developed, instead, an ability to kid himself into thinking that he can outsmart God. This scene is sinfully repeated every time one of us goes to the civil divorce courts to dissolve that which is in God's sight an indissoluble marriage. We hardly outsmart God! Instead, we only fool ourselves. Scripture is clear. If we then marry another, we commit adultery, because we are still married to the original partner. Marriage was designed to be permanent. It was this way from the very beginning, and it remains so today. The reason that so many of our good Christian friends divorce is that we have learned how to sin! Marriage's design hasn't changed—we have!

Another explanation for Christian divorce is that we have people who call themselves Christians but who have rehardened their hearts by rationalizing about their marriage difficulties to a point of confusion and disagreement with Scripture's teachings. They need help.

Counseling
Apart from those marriage difficulties that arise from a poor upbringing, neurotic or psychotic personalities, or emotional aberrations (all of which may require only a psychological approach), the key factor in bringing most couples back together is balanced counseling. Balanced counseling must be two-pronged—social and spiritual. One must recognize that some social *symptoms* (such as drunkenness, child beating, or even adultery) begin to appear publicly only after the primary wall of *spiritual* defense is lowered in the personal lives of those involved. This occurs when one ignores or abandons God. When spiritual barriers are thus lowered, social sins flourish. Now we have a two-headed monster to contend with, a spiritual problem and a social symptom, and it usually breathes the fire of divorce.

Surely counseling must include a Christ-centered social approach to treat the symptoms. But also there must be a Christ-centered spiritual emphasis to apply a healing touch to the disease itself, the disease which allowed the symptoms to flourish.

When a counselor concentrates only on the psychological and neglects the spiritual mending that is necessary to prevent recurrence, the couple involved is doomed for a double dose of the same affliction at a later date. Christ warns us of this: " 'When an evil spirit comes out of a man, it goes through arid places seeking rest and does not find it. Then it says, "I will return to the house I left." When it arrives, it finds the house swept clean and put in order. Then it goes and takes seven other spirits more wicked than itself, and they go in and live there. And the final condition of that man is worse than the first' " (Luke 11:24–26). Spiritual counseling, not just symptom-mending, is necessary to prevent further marital difficulties "worse than the first."

Obviously not all marriage counselors are dedicated to God's Word in an uncompromising allegiance, and some Christians know this. They make an effort to receive counseling, but they select a counselor who will tell them what they want to hear. The kind of counseling that ignores God's Word also ignores another fact: God often allows *marital pressures* to build as a reason to seek his solution. He doesn't need pastors, counselors, friends, or relatives blowing the lid off his pressure-cooker when he's busy softening hearts through marital pressures that are designed to lead couples to seek his help.

Because of this, there is a real urgency for all New Testament believers to become thoroughly versed in this subject. Only then can we share God's biblical view of marriage, divorce, and remarriage with those to whom he leads us. The story of Jesus Christ is the message we are to bring, just as Philip was called on to share his knowledge of the Scriptures with the Ethiopian eunuch. Philip opened his mouth "and told him the good news about Jesus" (Acts 8:35).

Who is qualified to counsel? One could suppose that the training necessary to properly equip a counselor is exactly that which is received in the seminary. But not all who graduate from the seminary are competent to counsel. The pastors and laymen who *are* competent are never *authorities* in their own right. Rather, a competent counselor is one who correctly handles the Word of Truth, reflecting the sovereign *authority* of Almighty God. Therefore, the competent counselors are, in my opinion, those pastors and Bible-based Christians who lean heavily and wholeheartedly on the Word of God for all their advice and guidance, and who have studied in depth God's absolute intention of indissolubility for marriage—*all* marriages.

Another reason for someone with a sound biblical background becoming involved with a couple in marital distress is that couple's spiritual vulnerability. If a struggling couple are left alone with only the coaxing of the devil, they may begin to think of divorce as a way to escape the kind of hell they are enduring. Many people are misguided by not being properly counseled and are misled by the popularity and frequency of the sin of divorce in our society today. It's becoming commonplace —even respectable in some circles—to divorce for the slightest provocation. A well-known national corporation has recently announced the adoption of a new policy regarding divorced persons. They state that an employee who sought a divorce is a person who had the stamina and fortitude to stand up to a bad situation and call the shots. They conclude that such a person thereby becomes executive material!

These notions are all around us. Television daytime dramas picture divorce as commonplace. But suppose that you or I were treated in a hospital the way marriage is treated on television. We'd die! For instance, imagine being in an accident, rushed to the hospital, and carted into emergency all battered up (the way some describe their marriages). A man walks in with no medical training, calling himself a doctor, and says, "This is a mess. For all practical purposes this patient is dead already. There are probably lots of hidden pressures building up also—causing other complications. He's beyond mending, impossible to save. Let's walk away from this, turn out the lights, and go home." Ridiculous? Not at all, when you consider that some counselors (without in-depth training in God's handbook for marriage) are actually *paid* for prescribing the sin of divorce for our troubled marriages.

I suppose that about now some reader will be thinking, "Hey, I am a Christian and already divorced. Is this book about what I *should* have done? Is it too late for me?" No! No to both questions. In later chapters I will discuss God's desire for those already divorced as well as those divorced and remarried. But for now, allow me to continue addressing those Christians presently faced only with the *temptation* to divorce. Take heart! God understands. He threatened his "wife" with a divorce more than once, and he actually did divorce her!

THREE
Israel and God:
Bride and Groom

"You adulterous wife! You prefer strangers to your own husband!" God declared to his bride in Ezekiel 16:32. God is married and his wife is bad news! Let's look at a few other things God said about his wife Israel: "Indeed, on every high hill and under every spreading tree you lay down as a prostitute" (Jeremiah 2:20). "How skilled you are at pursuing love! Even the worst of women can learn from your ways" (Jeremiah 2:33). "You have the brazen look of a prostitute" (Jeremiah 3:3b).

Sometimes we think our marriages are bad. But God's marriage to Israel was worse. Usually our marital problems arise out of sin by both parties. Not so with God's marriage. God is holy and faithful; his bride is a sinner and unfaithful. With that essential difference in mind, I take the liberty of referring to God's marriage as one having marital problems not unlike ours. God is the one perfect example of an *innocent* party in a marriage.

God had to take action. Read what God reluctantly did to his wife. "I gave faithless Israel her certificate of divorce and sent her away because of all her adulteries" (Jeremiah 3:8).

But then read what God said *after* the divorce (Jeremiah 3:12, 13):

> *"Return, faithless Israel," delares the Lord, "I will frown on you no longer, for I am merciful," declares the Lord, "I will not be angry forever. Only acknowledge your guilt —you have rebelled against the Lord your God, you have scattered your favors to foreign gods under every spreading tree, and have not obeyed me," declares the Lord.*

It is interesting to note that God divorced his wife for good cause, but then desired reconciliation more than revenge! Confess your sin, and I won't be angry, he told her. God hates divorce because his name is Reconcile (2 Corinthians 5:18–21).

Did God's marital problems end with the Israelites? No. We are a part of his continuing marital problems because as believers we belong to God through adoption and are married to Jesus Christ (John 1:12; 2 Corinthians 11:2). As Christians we are to have the mind of Christ and not be filled with sexual immorality, impurity, lusts, and evil desires. God lovingly tells us that he ascribes to us an *idolatrous* attitude when we entertain human desires (such as divorce) knowing that this ambition supplants his will for our lives (Galatians 5:2–21; 1 Corinthians 10:13, 14). Paul urges us to "put to death, therefore, whatever belongs to (our) earthly nature: sexual immorality, impurity, lusts, evil desires and greed, which is idolatry" (Colossians 3:5). Think of how often the sin of greed or sexual lusts go before a divorce. God is tenderly showing us that the idolatry his bride was (and continues to be) guilty of is far more than bowing down before the Old Testament's golden calf. Earthly desires—those out of harmony with God's will—are not only idle folly but idol worship.

Divorce, for reasons other than marital unfaithfulness, is an ineffective solution that transgresses God's will and purpose. We must reckon it as such if we are to be fair with God and ourselves. God, married to Israel, wanted us to know the anguish of his marital problems so that we might better understand the solution he offered his bride Israel. That solution is Jesus Christ!

To make his point unmistakably clear, God illustrated his marriage storm with Israel through the prophet Hosea 700 years before Christ, during an age of gross moral decay. God told Hosea to marry Gomer (a prostitute) and to have children with her. When she later willfully deserted him and committed adultery with her previous lovers, God commanded Hosea to go find her and take her back—as he had done with Israel. That's reconciliation! But Hosea not only had to find her and bring her back to himself, he had to *pay* money to get her back. He had to buy her back! Would you or I be willing to go that far in our reconciliatory duties? In commanding Hosea to do this, God pictured for us the true, rotten, and sinful condition of his bride *at the time* he married her; and in so doing, he foretold how Christ on the cross of Calvary would buy us all back.

Yet this beautiful fact seems to slip by so many Christians who are distraught with spiritual problems that cause marital conflict. Many feel they have it about as bad as anyone could have it. Yet they admit that at one time they thought marriage was a good idea—even exciting. But God took his bride in her most depressed condition, just as he took us "while we were still sinners" (Romans 5:8).

The saddest part of all this is that Israel's betrayal of God's love is repeated in each and every divorce between believers. They betray the power, grace, and love of God through Jesus Christ, all of which make a marriage work. Perhaps we might be able, in some small way, to imagine the humiliation of swallowing pride as Hosea was commanded to do (and did), but we are left totally incapable of comprehending the anguish and heartbreak that God, as the totally innocent party, had to endure for his bride Israel—and for us. But here is the good news: God is able to understand and appreciate the effort we take in accepting an unfaithful partner back. After all, he did more than just take us back. He *bought* us with his very blood!

Divorce is so sour in God's mouth that as the innocent party in this marital difficulty—involving adultery—he said to his wife:

> *"Return, O Israel, to the Lord your God. Your sins have been your downfall! . . . I will . . . love (you) freely, for my anger has turned away from (you)"* (Hosea 14:1, 4).

God continues to say to those of us who are troubled in our marriages: Be patient in the face of adverse conditions (Romans 5:3; James 1:3) and know that everything is in my hand under my control (Job 1:12, 2:6; Proverbs 21:1; Acts 17:25). God said through the Psalmist, "A righteous man may have many troubles, but the Lord delivers him from them all" (Psalm 34:19). Every last one of them! We know this will be the case since the Bible encourages each of us, along with Abraham, to be "fully persuaded that God (has) power to do what he had promised" (Romans 4:21). He's the God of marital miracles too!

So if you are in the middle of a marital struggle, one that is so severe that you think permanent scars will be left, or if you are about ready to throw in the towel, remember that our loving Father innocently suffered the full orb of marital mistreatment in its most rancid form and under the most unfair conditions. But being the great and wonderful God that he is, he has designed the perfect solution for us too: King Jesus! Jesus is the One who can write us a flawless prescription for our symptom of divorce—one that will rid us of the tricky notion that a divorce is a cure-all! Our problem isn't divorce, it's a refusal to trust Jesus Christ's prescription to soften our hearts. Isn't it tragic that as the heart becomes harder, it loses more of its ability to reconcile with anything or anyone—including God himself? Thus the urgency to listen to God's Word on divorce.

FOUR
God Says . . .

Because many of us have been so saddened by those who have had intolerable marital friction, I can understand why some Christians shrink from the uncompromising words of God about divorce. But because of sin and the fall of man, we cannot afford to do so. The Bible places divorce into four categories: 1) divorce between Christians, 2) divorce of a nonbeliever by a Christian, 3) divorce of a Christian by a nonbeliever, and 4) divorce between two nonbelievers.

But before we examine each category, allow me a few general statements regarding the indifference toward divorce in today's society. God's forthright command not to divorce seems forgotten by most people. It is a small, ignored part of our nation's spiritual consciousness, as are the words "In God We Trust." Few Americans realize the consequences of divorce, and many think it's nobody's business what happens to the couple down the street.

Yet before we come down too hard on others, we should admit that most of us Christians have a hard time including God in our own concept of marriage. To prove that point, ask several of your Christian friends, "Who married you?" Most will come right back with the name of the pastor, priest, or justice of the peace who stood before them and told them when to stand and kneel. Answers such as these betray our horizontal thinking when we are not alert to the real meaning behind the question, "Who married you?" In casual thinking, we all tend to leave God out of the very institution he formed and sealed.

In order to understand what divorce means to God, we must understand what in his design constitutes a marriage. Holy marriage is a divinely ordained institution which becomes a life-long bond between one male and one female as husband and wife. It is characterized by an intimate spiritual and physical (one-flesh) union. This holy, indissoluble union is sealed through a voluntary vow of mutual love and fidelity as God requires. The vow is taken before God, the originator of marriage, making him the sealer of every marriage union.

This definition does not allow the notion that sexual intercourse before marriage establishes a marriage union. Sexual activity after a marriage may consummate the marriage, but sex does not *establish* marriage. Likewise, this definition does not allow the notion that marital unfaithfulness (fornication or adultery) breaks the marriage bond. Sin does not have the capacity to destroy what God has created. Yet, unrepentant marital unfaithfulness can so severely damage a marital relationship that God does recognize a divorce (initiated by the offended, innocent party) as the only exception to his design for marriage.

Years ago, the word *divorce* made Christians think "vertically" and react *against* a marital course so contrary to God's purpose. But today the word divorce leads us to a more "horizontal" frame-of-reference. We ask questions such as, "Is the divorce final yet?" as though the government actually has the power to make a divorce. It may be said that the state *legalizes* marriages and divorces in order to avoid chaos and to protect all parties involved, including children, but this is not to say that God considers state-sanctioned divorce binding. He doesn't.

In and by itself the state does not establish a marriage. Therefore, if marriage does not owe its existence to the state (that is, if it is not established by the state), then the state cannot divorce people either. It is God alone who joins us together in Christian marriage. Governments only recognize (by making marriage legal) what God has instituted from the beginning. The Bible tells us, "Therefore what God has joined together, let man not separate" (Matthew 19:6). Man may not disjoin that which he had no function in joining in the first place. With that background, we can now look at the four categories of divorce as given in Scripture.

Divorce between Christians

Christians are not permitted to divorce or remarry after a divorce. God wisely provided guidelines for marriage, and not provisions for divorce and remarriage. Most of us realize this until we become involved in marital disharmony ourselves. God knows that! And he realizes that some Christians will "divorce" in spite of his warnings. That's why he laid it out so clearly for us. He said in effect, You think you can obtain a civil divorce for just any reason, but you really cannot! (Matthew 19:6). You will not be divorced at all (Matthew 19:9; Mark 10:11, 12); in fact, you are still married to your original partner until you are parted by death (1 Corinthians 7:39). And if you disobey, you will be committing adultery (Matthew 5:32; Luke 16:18). If two Christians do go to the civil divorce courts to obtain what they think is a real divorce, they are still commanded to be reconciled according to 1 Corinthians 7:10, 11: "To the married I give this command (not I, but the Lord): A wife must not separate from her husband. But if she does, she must remain unmarried or else be reconciled to her husband. And a husband must not divorce his wife." It's the same message all the way through the Scriptures. Short of marital unfaithfulness, all divorce attempts are invalid! This is true regardless of who seeks the divorce—the husband or the wife. This is vividly told us in Mark 10:11, 12: "Anyone who divorces his wife and marries another woman commits adultery against her. And if she divorces her husband and marries another man, she commits adultery."

The Bible leaves absolutely no room for misinterpretation. Those going through the motions of a civil divorce only fool themselves, not God, into thinking they are now single. They, like Adam, have fallen victim to a heinous ploy of the devil. Not only have they been duped and tricked into thinking they have found real freedom apart from Christ, but they have just been fooled into publicly denying and rejecting the power, love, and promises of Jesus, their Savior.

Those are strong terms, "denying and rejecting . . . Jesus." You may ask, "Is divorce really *that* serious?"

It is!

A Christian who seeks a divorce denies Christ's lordship. Let's examine that statement in the light of Scripture. The most detailed account of marriage and divorce in the Bible is recorded for us in Matthew's Gospel (19: 3–9). "Some Pharisees came to him to test him. They asked, 'Is it lawful for a man to divorce his wife for any and every reason?' 'Haven't you read,' he replied, 'that at the beginning the Creator "made them male and female," and said, "For this reason a man will leave his father and mother and be united to his wife, and the two will become one flesh?" So they are no longer two, but one. Therefore what God has joined together, let man not separate.' 'Why then,' they asked, 'did Moses command that a man give his wife a certificate of divorce and send her away?' Jesus replied, 'Moses permitted you to divorce your wives because your hearts were hard. But it was not this way from the beginning. I tell you that anyone who divorces his wife, except for marital unfaithfulness, and marries another woman commits adultery.' "

I would like to consider this passage verse by verse and demonstrate how this denial and rejection of the lordship of our loving Savior accompanies every Christian's attempt to divorce.

Verse 3 reads, "Some Pharisees came to him to test him. They asked, 'Is it lawful for a man to divorce his wife for any and every reason?' " The Pharisees were not followers of Christ, so they designed the question to begin a dispute. They did not desire to be taught; they unmistakably posed the question to trick him. Christ's answer to the Pharisees' question was given in the form of another question, "Haven't you read . . . ?" It's sobering to think that Christians today, contemplating divorce, ask much the same question. It must sadden God terribly. Such a desire ignores the sovereignty of God and at the same time demonstrates a lack of desire to learn God's will for their lives.

Jesus' answer would be the same today. "Haven't you read . . . ?" Haven't you read your Bible? Or if you have, did you consider it, study it, and pray to be enlightened by it? Our Lord did not give a yes or no answer. Why not? Because the question was a trap. If Christ had answered no, the Pharisees could then have accused him of being an enemy of Moses' law, which allowed divorce. If he would have answered yes, the Pharisees could have accused him of being lax. So instead of a yes or no answer, Jesus answers them (and us) with a question of his own in verse 4. " 'Haven't you read,' he replied, 'that at the beginning the Creator "made them male and female," and said, "For this reason a man will leave his father and mother and be united to his wife . . ." '?"

What was our Lord saying here? I think he was reminding us of the fact that the male and female identity is rooted in God's original creation. God envisioned in creation the close and intimate union of one man and one woman in marriage. Jesus emphasized that point in verse 4. He might also be saying to us, Remember that Eve was taken from a rib of Adam; so even if Adam *could* divorce Eve, he would be putting away part of himself as well. This is a fact of life for all married couples today! We become one flesh, and God says, "Husbands ought to love their wives as their own bodies. He who loves his wife loves himself" (Ephesians 5:28, 29). Still another implication is that marriage as God ordained it, and sex as God created it, are among the highest, holiest, and happiest gifts God has bestowed on his creatures.

Verse 5 spells this out further: " 'For this reason a man will leave his father and mother and be united to his wife, and the two will become one flesh.' " For which reason? The intimacy of one male and one female united in the permanency of the marriage bond! For *that* reason a man will leave the natural attachment to father and mother for a deeper, more binding union with his wife.

Christ is instructing us that the union between a husband and wife is much closer than that which either had with his or her parents. Granted, the parent-child relationship is an extremely intimate one, but that's the whole point Jesus is making: marriage is an *even deeper* bond which cannot be broken for just "any and every reason" (Matthew 19:3). As children, we are the genes and chromosomes of our parents; that is, we are *parts* of them. In marriage we become *one* with our partner. This makes marriage indissoluble and divorce as impracticable as it is biblically forbidden!

Verse 6 continues this thought and nails it home. "So they are no longer two, but one. Therefore what God has joined together, let man not separate." Here is God's clear-cut divine command *not* to divorce! It is a command given to all men, churched or unchurched, believer or unbeliever, to all husbands and wives, governments, and churches. Our Lord is saying here that all couples are united by God for life. "A woman is bound to her husband as long as he lives," God said through Paul in 1 Corinthians 7:39. There is no divine permission for man to interfere. In another way our Lord is saying, Now that you are one flesh, joined by God, don't be tricked into thinking that you, or your earthly court systems, can change that divine fact. "What God has joined together, let man not separate."

This leads us to the next trap the Pharisees set for our Lord. Remembering the words of Moses, they asked in Matthew 19:7, "Why then . . . did Moses command that a man give his wife a certificate of divorce and send her away?" Grasp the blasphemy that lies behind the Pharisees' question! It was framed to accomplish two things. First, to indicate that possibly Jesus hadn't studied the Scriptures completely himself. Second, to expose what they considered to be a contradiction between God's Word and this man's teaching; namely, "What God has joined together, let man not separate." (They had read Moses on the subject in Deuteronomy 24:1 where it says, "If a man marries a woman who becomes displeasing to him because he finds something indecent about her, [let him write] her a certificate of divorce, [give] it to her, and [send her away].") They retorted: "Why then . . . did Moses command that a man give his wife a certificate of divorce and send her away?"

Especially note their use of the word *command*. Our Lord was quick to pick up the violation of terminology in his direct answer in verse 8. "Jesus replied, 'Moses permitted you to divorce your wives because your hearts were hard." But it was not this way in the beginning, and there *never was a command to divorce*.

Perhaps the most important words are "your hearts were hard," because it is right here that our Lord sums up the singular cause (not an excuse or grounds) for all divorce: hardened hearts—a turning away from God. As I said before, this was no compliment. It is precisely at this point that our Lord established the shocking realization that for many Christians living today, divorce means denying and rejecting his lordship in their lives. He says in effect, The law of Moses took into consideration the hardness of man's heart. But the gospel I preach cures and prevents that sickness.

Christ's presence in our hearts prevents hardened hearts. Christ has conquered sin, fulfilled the law for us, and his Holy Spirit's indwelling is now a softening agent to prevent the rehardening of the redeemed heart.

A second time Jesus redirects our attention to the beginning of time—the days of creation before the fall when he said, "It was not this way in the beginning" (v. 8). Hardened hearts did not exist, nor did fornication or adultery. They resulted from the fall, and our Lord recognizes them in verse 9. "I tell you that anyone who divorces his wife, except for marital unfaithfulness, and marries another woman commits adultery." The word "anyone" includes Christian and non-Christian alike, just as it included the Pharisees and all of mankind in Jesus' day. Jesus said, "I tell you that anyone who divorces his wife . . . and marries another woman commits adultery." Many misread verse 9 by assuming that divorce is something God expects will happen anyway, and by emphasizing the words, "and marries another . . ." many conclude that a divorce is acceptable to God as long as one does not remarry.

This is not the way to read God's Word. One may not consider verse 9 at the expense of verse 8, which just recited for the second time that from the beginning of time divorce was *not* God's way. Jesus is not saying that divorce is a lesser sin than remarriage. Rather, our Lord recognizes that some will try to divorce *in spite of* his New Testament warnings. When they do this, they will be denying Christ's lordship first, themselves second, and their partner last. Believers simply may not divorce. If they disobey, they set themselves up to "commit adultery." Paul writes, "By law a married woman is bound to her husband as long as he is alive, but if her husband dies, she is released from the law of marriage. So then, if she marries another man while her husband is still alive she is called an adulteress. But if her husband dies, she is released from that law and is not an adulteress, even though she marries another man" (Romans 7:2, 3).

Consider how this entire conversation between Christ and the Pharisees began. They had asked, "Is it lawful for a man to divorce his wife for any and every reason?" Jesus answered their question straight and to the point in verse 9. In doing so, he threw out all notions that he might provide guidelines for divorce. Note how our Lord carefully avoids labeling fornication (marital unfaithfulness) as a *ground* for divorce. The exceptive clause ("except for marital unfaithfulness") serves only to qualify God's intent for marriage and is not something Jesus gave as grounds for a divorce. I will have more to say about the exceptive clause in chapter 6 of this book.

In summary, two believers may not divorce or remarry unless there is marital unfaithfulness (fornication) present. I am aware of the existence of many questions in the reader's mind about extenuating circumstances. I will deal with these questions in chapters 5 and 7 of this book.

Divorce of a Nonbeliever by a Christian
Divorce is not allowed between a believer and an unbeliever if the non-Christian wishes to remain married to the Christian. Paul explains this for us with these words: "If any brother has a wife who is not a believer and she is willing to live with him, he must not divorce her. And if a woman has a husband who is not a believer

and he is willing to live with her, she must not divorce him" (1 Corinthians 7:12, 13).

But it's precisely in those times of marital tension that we raise the question, "Why must disharmony continue just because the unbeliever doesn't want to leave?" Paul answers this query in 1 Corinthians 7:14—"For the unbelieving husband has been sanctified through the wife, and the unbelieving wife has been sanctified through her believing husband. Otherwise your children would be unclean, but as it is, they are holy."

Here God is giving us a series of extremely important facts. Marital relationships are sanctified by the spirituality of either partner. Therefore, divorce is forbidden. In other words, if one partner is "holy" the entire marriage is holy in God's sight. "Otherwise your children would be unclean, but as it is, they [too] are holy" (1 Corinthians 7:14b).

Let's note the three advantages in a marriage where one partner is a believer. Not only are the children holy in God's sight, but they are declared a part of the covenant. Of equal importance is the believer's built-in opportunity to influence the unbeliever's eternal destiny. Finally, the unbeliever is actually sanctified through the believer as Paul states in 1 Corinthians 7:14.

I am sure that some readers will have a serious problem picturing their unbelieving partner as one who is sanctified, especially if he or she curses God, physically mistreats spouse and children, doesn't share in responsibilities, is unemployed or lazy most of the time, and perhaps even a drunkard. Yet, if you are a Christian your unbelieving partner *is* sanctified, and, according to our all-wise God, if he or she does not want a divorce, you are prohibited from obtaining one.

God illustrates his reason for demanding this in these words: "How do you know, wife, whether you will save your husband? Or, how do you know, husband, whether you will save your wife?" (1 Corinthians 7:16). When

Christ was on earth, Nicodemus had difficulty understanding the concept of the second birth. Jesus told him:
"You should not be surprised at my saying 'you must be
born again.' The wind blows wherever it pleases. You
hear its sound, but you cannot tell where it comes from
or where it is going. So it is with everyone born of the
Spirit" (John 3:7, 8). So to each believer married to an
unbeliever (who may be causing problems but not seeking a divorce), God says in effect, How do you know,
wife, where my Spirit's wind will blow? I might save
your husband through your witness to him. Or, how do
you know, husband, whether I am going to save your
wife through your demonstration of my love in and
through your marriage difficulties?

If the nonbeliever wishes to remain married, the believer may not divorce. I know this is difficult for some
to accept, and nearly impossible for others who are involved in a soul-shaking marital failure where uniden-
tified flying objects make partners duck more often than
they'd like. But God doesn't drop it there either. He is
as practical as he is demanding, and we will consider
some biblical practicalities in the next chapter.

Divorce of a Christian by a Nonbeliever
Here we have an entirely different situation. Separation
(not divorce) *is* permitted between a believer and an
unbeliever if the *unbeliever* insists on it. However, we
must be careful not to read too much or too little into
this. The source for this is found in 1 Corinthians 7:15
where Paul says, "But if the unbeliever leaves, let him do
so. A believing man or woman is not bound in such
circumstances; God has called us to live in peace."

Part of the caution here arises from the fact that
Paul addressed those couples who were *married as unbelievers* but later one became a Christian. This limits
the application. There are three possible observations

that nevertheless come to light in this context.

First, in the early Corinthian church Christianity was relatively new. There had been a good response to the gospel message and some individuals had been converted. What began as equally yoked marriages were now unequally yoked due to the conversion of just one partner. The other partner no doubt wondered about the dramatic change that took place. In this regard, Paul's words in 1 Corinthians 7:15 are as applicable today as then.

A second perspective might be made. If two people, thought to be Christians, marry, and one of them later confesses (or is found) to be an unbeliever, the situation might parallel the first case. It is conceivable to me that God might include such victims of an *unknown* unequally yoked marriage within the same spirit of 1 Corinthians 7:15. I will develop this thought further in the next chapter.

The third and most important point I wish to make is that 1 Corinthians 7:15 does *not* apply to a Christian who knowingly and disobediently marries an unbeliever. All believers are clearly warned *not* to be unequally yoked to known unbelievers. This warning applies to many areas of life, but surely to marriage. It is found in 2 Corinthians 6:14 where we read, "Do not be yoked together with unbelievers. For what do righteousness and wickedness have in common?" Therefore, a believer must never consciously enter into an unequally yoked marriage with an unbeliever.

In the example before us, Paul says, "If the unbeliever leaves, let him do so. A believing man or woman is not bound in such circumstances; God has called us to live in peace." Paul is not contradicting what our Lord said in Matthew 19:3–9. Paul is not giving us a loophole here, or any other excuse that changes what was previously established by God from the beginning. Moses *permitted* divorce because God's people had hardened their hearts, and Paul is recognizing the same hardness of heart in the unbeliever in the New Testament. If a New Testament *unbeliever* insists upon leaving a marital relationship with a believer, it is obvious that the unbeliever has not been influenced by Christ's Spirit, nor by the believer's faith or witness. So, because of his unbelieving heart, let him depart. This is sad, but it represents nothing new about hardened hearts. Only faith in Jesus Christ and the power of his Holy Spirit can soften a hard heart.

Have you ever wondered what the word "bound" really meant? The verb "bound" in the original Greek is *dedoulōtai.* The term can be translated "is not enslaved." It means something different from what most assume. Many read it here in 1 Corinthians 7:15 and conclude that the believer is not bound to the marriage any longer and may therefore divorce—even remarry. But when the Bible speaks of that kind of "bound," as in 1 Corinthians 7:39 ("A woman is bound to her husband as long as he lives"), the original word for "bound" is *dedetai.* These words in the original are not the same in verses 15 and 39 of 1 Corinthians 7. The question then arises, Might the different words mean the same thing? Some argue that they do. They point to the same problem with some of our English words, such as "doorway" and "exit." These, too, are different words but essentially mean the same thing. Others maintain there is an inherent difference here and that they mean something different in each case. Obviously, the word "bound" in verse 39 means the marriage bond ("A woman is bound to her husband as long as he lives"). But in verse 15 I do not believe that the word "bound" means the marriage bond. It says, "A believing man or woman is not bound in such circumstances . . . ." I feel it refers to the *bondage (or obligation) of the believer to witness to the unbeliever, or reconcile with him or her.* The believer, in verse 15, is exempted from those marriage *duties,* but not from the marriage.

Because the two verbs are different (even though they

are from the same basic Greek root and etymologically related), they may well have different meanings. I do not believe Scripture allows us to assume that a deserted believer is automatically single and free to remarry, nor that the desertion is a ground for divorce. Such an assumption would be difficult to make in light of verse 39 and other portions of Scripture that imply otherwise. (Cf. Romans 7:2, 3; Matthew 5:32, 19:9; and Mark 10:11, 12.)

When someone has a question about remarriage and searches the Scripture for an *explicit* answer, the only uncontested situation we find for a marriage being broken is when one of the partners dies. Even then, interestingly enough, permission to remarry can only be interpreted as being offered reluctantly. Paul said, "In my judgment, she is happier if she stays as she is—and I think that I too have the Spirit of God" (1 Corinthians 7:40). (Contested remarriages will be dealt with in chapter 9.)

Therefore, in this light we conclude two things: separation (not divorce) is allowed in verse 15, and celibacy (not remarriage) is expected after the unbeliever leaves. Departing, in and of itself, is not grounds for divorce anywhere in Scripture.

An exception to all of this would again be if the unbeliever remarried. The believer could then recognize the existence of adultery in the remarriage of the unbeliever and claim the exceptive clause of Matthew's Gospel.

Divorce Between Two Unbelievers
Success in marriage is spelled J-E-S-U-S A-S L-O-R-D. Unbelievers can, at best, only imitate a successful marriage since only the Holy Spirit is capable of softening mankind's naturally hard heart.

The Bible does not speak directly to the subject of divorce between two unbelievers; however, our Lord's implications regarding the question are clear. Even though God permitted the people of the Old Testament to divorce (because of their hardened hearts), it is clear that it was not God's perfect will. Unbelievers will divorce for all sorts of reasons. They will marry, divorce, and remarry often because of their Christless egos. Ego typifies all hardened hearts. It is pure grace that some unbelievers do stay married.

But too often when the Church becomes vocal about the rate of divorce in the world it begins to speak out against divorce as though it were unnatural. That's not true! It's the *Christian* who is unnatural. God speaks of three kinds of people: the natural unredeemed man, the worldly self-relying Christian, and the Christ-centered spiritual Christian who relies wholly upon Jesus. As God's redeemed, we must bear testimony to his solution to sin. The world really doesn't need the Church to condemn it for its widespread divorce. The world needs Jesus Christ for its heart problem!

If we would proclaim the saving power of Jesus Christ as often as we condemn divorce, the divorce rate would drop. Did you know that 38 percent of all first marriages end in divorce in America? Did you know that in 1978 there were 1,120,000 divorces involving 1,122,000 innocent children? While 80 percent of those questioned maintained that they should have only one wife, only 33 percent felt that marriage should last a lifetime. Yet statistically 62 percent remained married until parted by death.

There's cause for alarm in these statistics, but also hope. The alarm is that as Christians, entrusted with the holy Scriptures, we are losing the battle. The divorce rate has multiplied seven times since the 1900s and doubled since 1968! Time is running out. The hope is that we have the solution to tell them. Only Christ's Spirit can make a person able to survive with his partner and God.

Therefore, one of the chief problems with the world's divorce rate is the Christian who is not proclaiming Jesus Christ as the cure for the evils of divorce. Isn't that how God would rather have us tackle the problem? "For God did not send his Son into the world to condemn the world, but to save the world through him" (John 3:17).

We have now covered the four biblical categories of divorce as the Bible gives them to us. However, God didn't stop there. He also has some practical pointers for us to consider. Let's look at a typical case.

FIVE
A Practical Case

I could pick any one of a dozen social sins that damage marital relationships, but I choose one of the worst: physical abuse. Physical abuse is probably more common in Christian marriages than most of us realize. What does a Christian do in such a situation?

Imagine a nice looking married couple who attend church faithfully, have been known in the church since their birth, and were married within its sanctuary. At the time of their marriage, the husband professed to be a Christian, so everyone properly assumed they were equally yoked. Though he claims to be a fine Christian husband, actually he is an unbeliever and a wife-beater, admitting to neither. Jesus, quoting Isaiah, said of these kinds of people, "[They] honor me with their lips, but their hearts are far from me" (Matthew 15:8).

The best place to go with this situation is to the church. Why the church? Because one of two things is going to happen. Either the pretender will be converted, or he will be officially judged an unbeliever in the course of church discipline. Therefore, if one partner truly suspects the other partner to be an unbeliever (after the marriage has taken place) and sees no progress in attempts to eliminate the physical abuse, save him, or save the marriage, the best course of action is to bring it to the church.

One might suspect that a legal separation is an alternative, but many attorneys feel the courts would no longer honor that approach. And so they advise, "If you want to keep your partner out of the house, file for a divorce." Thus the problem: how can a wife deal with this situation? It is impossible for her to stay with her husband, yet it is impermissible to divorce.

Let me say right here that I do not believe anyone has direct scriptural answers, but I do believe there are some logical scriptural implications that address themselves to these situations. We can begin with the specific biblical data that is available to us, and work from there.

First, if *believers* separate (of their own accord—not a legal separation), they are commanded to "remain unmarried or else be reconciled . . ." (1 Corinthians 7:11). Second, if an unbeliever departs, the believer is allowed to let him leave and is *not* under bondage to reconcile, as is stated in 1 Corinthians 7:15. But the man in my example *claims to be a Christian,* so we must work from that premise.

The church is extremely important here. There are theological aspects to the social problem of physical abuse also. The church is important because of these spiritual implications and because it holds the keys to the kingdom of heaven. God tells us in Matthew 18:15–18, "If your brother sins against you, go and show him his fault, just between the two of you. If he listens to you, you have won your brother over. But if he will not listen, take one or two others along, so that 'every matter may be established by the testimony of two or three witnesses.' If he refuses to listen to them [and I assume the believer to have followed these instructions to this point], tell it to the church; and if he refuses to listen even to the church, treat him as you would a pagan or a tax collector. I tell you the truth, whatever you bind on earth will be bound in heaven, and whatever you loose on earth will be loosed in heaven." After the wife has confronted her husband with the problem, and brought in others as witnesses to the problem, Jesus tells her to *tell it to the Church.*

Here is some more of the problem: if this physically abused wife is married to a believer, she may not divorce or separate, according to the Bible. If she is married to an unbeliever, the couple may separate (according to Scripture), though only if the unbeliever voluntarily leaves.

The question now becomes focused: Do we or do we not know for sure (in a concrete case) that someone is not a believer? It is going to be very difficult to judge the heart of someone who claims to be a Christian (with the facade to back that up) but is suspected to be just the opposite.

We can agree, I assume, that the prime difficulty in such a marriage is the lack of commitment to Jesus Christ on the part of the unbeliever. We can also agree that either the evil influences on that person must be eliminated—possibly through a conversion—or the person will have to be disassociated or excommunicated from the church. To accomplish the latter we would have to involve the official church so that he may be officially declared an unbeliever, and in doing so, pray that the former will happen instead.

Meanwhile, what about the threat of physical abuse? Here the church can supply a practical solution by placing the abused wife in the home of a member of the church, and thus accomplish a safe separation while the elders work with the offending husband. However, under no circumstances may we *compel* desertion or advise divorce, nor *assume* he is an unbeliever without the church so declaring.

I wonder if some readers might be thinking that I have

now become as technical as the Pharisees were in their questioning Christ about the proper way to get rid of someone, or that I ought rather to concentrate on the right way to help this couple remain happily married in the Lord. But there is good reason for addressing these technicalities. Remember, we are considering two "professing Christians" who are in deep marital difficulty—wanting to separate, perhaps even divorce, but who lack scriptural warrant to do so. The only *obvious* biblical answers are Matthew 5:32, 19:9; Mark 10:11, 12; and Luke 16:18, which all say, No divorce permitted! On the other hand, we may properly raise the question in the case of physical abuse: "Is this the way God intended married couples to live together?"

A pastor once asked me, "Don't you think that God ever looks the other way in certain cases where there is either a disastrous mismatch or terrible hurt involved?" Perhaps the pastor had something like physical abuse in mind when he asked the question. Does God ever disregard divorce? Do you think he does? If you answer in the affirmative, you might be thought of as permissive. On the other hand, if you answer with a no, the person asking the question might be led into needless frustrations and pointless hurts. *God does offer solutions!* Christians need never feel locked into physical abuse (or any distasteful marital relationship) and thus locked out of the physical, emotional, and spiritual bliss that God desires for every marriage. Just as we are advised to look at *all* of Scripture without applying any text out of context, we must now also look at the total biblical picture of what God expects of two married people who are having personal troubles.

The fact that these partners may have grown up inside the walls of the church together does not, in itself, guarantee that either is a true believer. The fact that this unbeliever professes to be a Christian does not, of itself, certify that he is born again. Jesus said, "Not everyone who says to me, 'Lord, Lord,' will enter the kingdom of heaven, but only he who does the will of my Father who is in heaven" (Matthew 7:21). Our Lord went even further: "Many will say to me on that day, 'Lord, Lord, did we not prophesy in your name, and in your name drive out demons and perform many miracles?' Then I will tell them plainly, 'I never knew you. Away from me, you evildoers!' " (Matthew 7:22, 23). If a man does not live the Christian life day by day, then his church attendance only proves that he was present, nothing else. A mouth full of empty words is just that—the words are empty, and as such they are abominable to God.

Once I had a man tell me and several friends how he became born again. Sitting together in my living room we shared in his beautiful testimony, one you could hardly doubt—and I didn't. Later he absconded with a great deal of my money. His words were meaningless, and I had judged him only on his words. Jesus told us, "By their fruit you will recognize them" (Matthew 7:20). God never said that all within the Church are sons of God, nor that everyone faithfully attending his Church is a true believer, nor that mere words or outward appearances accurately reflect the inner heart. He's more practical than that. And this physically abusing husband may not be a born-again person at all (and in my example he is not), but who are we to accurately judge?

Are any of us in a position to do the judging alone? How could one Christian partner judge the spiritual lack of life in the other? Indeed, there are biblical texts forbidding us to censure each other rashly (Matthew 7:1; 1 Corinthians 4:3). Yet the Bible also speaks of another kind of judging in order to properly determine a cause or to rightly discern (Exodus 18:13; 1 Corinthians 2:15).

If Christ meant for Christians to judge each other when he said, "By their fruit you will recognize them" (Matthew 7:20), then who may do the judging even in the Church? Paul answers that for us with these words:

"The spiritual man makes judgments about all things" (1 Corinthians 2:15). To make that more specific, Christ established the Church to oversee the application of his Holy Word. Paul said it this way: "To the elders among you, I appeal as a fellow elder. . . . Be shepherds of God's flock . . . serving as overseers" (1 Peter 5:1, 2). The God-given duty of the elders to judge others with discernment is also spelled out for us in Acts 15:2, 1 Timothy 5:17, Titus 1:5, and James 5:14. It's the elders within the official church who can judge with spiritual discernment. What they bind on earth will be bound in heaven (Matthew 18:18).

Regretfully, many people in situations such as this don't seem to want to go to the church at this late date. The basic reason for this is that they consider their marriage already terminal. "Why go to the church? It's hopeless." Others prefer not to make ripples or rash statements that could be self-damaging; they are still trying to hold on to their facade. At the earlier stages there are many who do not want rumors started about their marriage. They consider "the less said, the better" and secretly suffer while their marriage worsens. And then it *is* nearly too late! One should always come to God's people early. But the wife in my example knows that she does not have biblical support for a divorce, and this may be one of the reasons the church is not sought out early.

Perhaps I could further justify such a technical analysis of the problem. In the late stages of any marital difficulty, neither party is likely to consider the actual *spiritual problem* present; that is, they are by then fully convinced that their only problem is marital. They are no longer able to recognize the basic spiritual disease, and therefore they do not actively seek a spiritual cure. Now, if a "cold," objective, technical analysis should become the catalyst to move them toward the church, all the better. Once they come to the church, the necessary corrective measures will be instituted.

Following the specifics of my example a little further, the church will no doubt begin to deal with the *problem* (the inconsistencies of the husband's spiritual life) which are now properly and officially in front of them. Bringing it to the church is the first step in any solution.

Church leaders may never act rashly! Discipline may begin, but its purpose is never to excommunicate or disassociate someone; rather, the goal of all church discipline is to evangelize and restore. Therefore, the church may begin redemptive discipline with the husband, or maybe even husband and wife, in an effort to restore them to spiritual health and full communion with our Lord.

Aside from what may have prompted them to move toward the church, God's healing ministry (through the work of the elders) should begin at the first hint of spiritual or marital discord. God's Word commands this. "Tell it to the church; and if he refuses to listen even to the church, treat him as you would a pagan (unbeliever) or a tax collector" (Matthew 18:17). Jesus Christ said those words: *tell it to the church!*

If the husband in my example does not respond to the church's redemptive admonition, a stricter punitive discipline must then be initiated and enforced by the elders of the church. This is one of the many roles that the Church on earth is forced to perform in the name of God. He instructs his Church—as the spiritually strong —to "preach the word; be prepared in season and out of season; correct, rebuke and encourage—with great patience and careful instruction" (2 Timothy 4:2). But when a person rejects the efforts of Christ's body, the Church is forced to purge itself of that troublemaker. Again, this is God's command to the Church, not something the Church thought up to harass someone with a nearly perfect facade. God instructs us in this way: "Warn a divisive person once, and then warn him a second time. After that, have nothing to do with him"

(Titus 3:10). This is God's way today, as it was in the Old Testament when he said, "A man who remains stiff-necked after many rebukes will suddenly be destroyed—without remedy" (Proverbs 29:1).

Assuming the church declares this husband (who once claimed to be a believer) an unbeliever, and assuming he wants to leave the marriage, *then* the believing wife may claim the peace offered in 1 Corinthians 7:15. However, this wife is still under the obligation not to marry another.

If the unbeliever decides to stay, the believer is commanded to comply with this decision and maintain the marriage, according to 1 Corinthians 7:12, 13. But if the situation is still physically or spiritually threatening to the believer or her family, a temporary separation is allowed, again providing that the words of Scripture are applied as found in 1 Corinthians 7:11, 14.

Of special importance is the point that one may not merely assume that the other is not a Christian, nor assume someone to be a candidate for disassociation or excommunication from the church. This is not a matter for an individual to determine. Nor may any of us proceed to encourage someone, such as the husband in my example, to depart as an unbeliever until God (through the Church) verifies the fallen condition of this "professing Christian." We may never jump ahead of God and bypass the Church, for in so doing we ignore the real purpose behind all church discipline: Christ's love.

I had a man say to me once, "You're impractical! By the time the church wheels turn in a crisis the worst has already happened. In the case of this poor wife, by the time the church acted, she might have been killed!" Well, he forgot the possibility of a swift and safe physical separation. He also forgot that God is very much interested in treating both the cause and the symptom of a crisis. "Spinning wheels" is *really* treating the symptom while not treating the cause. Then, nothing gets accomplished. Or, the wrong thing gets accomplished.

Paul chides every Christian who may question the necessity of going to the Church or the Church's authority with these words: "Do you not know that we will judge angels? How much more the things of this life!" (1 Corinthans 6:3). How much *more,* he said, the things of this life.

Remember the question the pastor posed earlier? "Don't you think that God ever looks the other way in certain cases where there is either a disastrous mismatch or terrible hurt involved?" Isn't the answer now obvious? God doesn't have to overlook anything, since he has already provided for every possibility in Scripture and may, through church discipline, be providing for a conversion or restoration instead of a divorce. God *is* as practical as he is demanding!

Marital disasters caused by factors other than adultery or fornication, such as the example we just considered, are tricky enough to handle. You would think that the obvious sin of fornication and the exceptive clause would be easier to handle; but get ready for a shocker! The subject of fornication, as detailed for us in Matthew's Gospel, is very involved and deeply intriguing. Matthew 5:32 and 19:9 are perhaps the most quoted and least understood verses about divorce in the Bible.

SIX
The Exceptive Clause

If you were to ask most Christians, "What in your opinion is the one thing God would recognize as a reason for a divorce in the Bible?" the majority would answer, "Adultery." They take as their authority the "exceptive clause" in Matthew 19:9, ". . . except for marital unfaithfulness. . . ."

But few Christians clearly understand the real meaning of marital unfaithfulness (as the *New International Version* translates *porneia*) or fornication (as some older translations render *porneia*). I want to caution the reader that I will freely interchange the English terms fornication and marital unfaithfulness since both are translated from the same original word *porneia*. For my purposes then, fornication and marital unfaithfulness are the same sin. However, neither is the same as adultery *(moicheia)*. There is a difference between adultery and fornication —a point I take from our Lord's statement where he used both words in the same sentence. He said, "I tell you that anyone who divorces his wife, except for marital unfaithfulness, and marries another woman commits adultery" (Matthew 19:9). "Except for *marital unfaithfulness* . . . commits *adultery*," he said. What is the difference between marital unfaithfulness (fornication) and adultery? What do you think fornication means?

The term is a confusing one, and going to the dictionary is of little help since today's dictionaries explain fornication as "voluntary sexual intercourse between *unmarried* persons" (italics mine). That doesn't sound like *marital* unfaithfulness! Adultery, on the other hand, means "sexual intercourse between a married person and another not the spouse." The question must then be asked, "Was Jesus thinking of fornication as something reserved for singles (as Webster defines the word) when he gave us the exceptive clause—the exception to God's design for marriage?" There are those who maintain that the fornication to which Christ was referring could have been fornication committed prior to the marriage. I prefer not to debate that here.

Still there had to be a good reason why Jesus used two different terms in one sentence. There must be a difference. Fornication consists of much more than adultery. I believe it *includes* adultery, to be sure; but it also includes prostitution, sodomy, homosexuality, incest, and all other forms of sexual uncleanness which could better be called marital unfaithfulness. This would mean that *all* adultery is fornication, but all fornication is not necessarily strictly limited to the category of adultery.

God realizes that fornication, in any of its forms, violates the one-flesh bond of marriage. Fornication, and all the disharmony that results from it, often carries with it irreversible emotional, physical, mental, social, and spiritual consequences. The sin of fornication disavows the core purpose and function of any marriage. The word "fornication" is used twenty-two times in the New Testament describing various kinds of illicit sexual relationships. These include, but are not limited to, adultery.

Jesus seems to be saying in Matthew 19:9 and 5:32 that because the effect of this sin is so radical and horrendous, God may permit (not command) an exception to his own edict not to divorce. The reason I say *may* is because we must bear in mind the context surrounding our Lord's statement. The Pharisees had asked if "it (was) lawful for a man to divorce his wife for any and every reason" (Matthew 19:3). Christ's answer was a reaffirmation of the permanency of marriage; that is, its indissolubility. Christ's purpose in giving us the exceptive clause was not to give us grounds for divorce. The exceptive clause serves only as a qualification of Jesus' emphatic and well-attested teaching that *marriage after divorce constitutes adultery!* None of us knows exactly why Jesus mentions *porneia* as the exceptive circumstance. We can only guess that physical infidelity (marital unfaithfulness) symbolizes that which strikes at the very heart of the marriage relationship. However, we may not conclude that fornication *breaks* a marriage. The point I wish to make here is that, in the presence of fornication, one has reason to feel violated, sure, but to go beyond that and state that this is a biblically approved ground for divorce is to read more into the text than what our Lord actually said. Even in the face of having been deeply hurt, we may never forget the overriding and constant theme of Scripture: reconciliation!

In order to grasp our Lord's intent, we must look again at the context surrounding his statement and exception. We know that the Pharisees were trying to trick him into taking sides with either the liberal or conservative school of thought on divorce. When he instead reestablished God's original intent for marriage by saying, "Therefore what God has joined together, let man not separate" (Matthew 19:6b), the Pharisees threw Moses' divorce laws at him. With his answer in Matthew 19:9 our Lord eliminated all man-made excuses for divorce, including those the Pharisees were quibbling about, declaring all of Moses' allowances completely null and void. Christ's purpose in even mentioning divorce was to make the point that from the beginning divorce was not acceptable to God. He was not establishing a ground for divorce per se.

Therefore, if we are to be honest with the Scriptures, we will have to agree that the exceptive clause serves only as a *possible* allowance for an *exceptional* divorce recognized by God. Don't misunderstand me. I personally feel that if fornication is present and unrepented (this would imply that it is also repeated) there is biblical justification for the innocent partner to seek a divorce. The point is that Christ's intention with the exceptive clause was not to offer a ground for divorce but rather an argument for marriage. Jesus was speaking of the permanency of marriage in Matthew 5:32 and 19:9.

There are three specifics of Jesus' exceptive clause that come to light: 1) We may safely assume that Christ wanted us to recognize that only one party was guilty in the exceptive situation he cited. The other partner was absolutely innocent—not unlike the innocent bridegroom, God, and his guilty bride, Israel. 2) We *can* disobey God and obtain a false divorce from the worldly courts. He said "Anyone who divorces . . . ," recognizing that some will divorce in spite of his command not to divorce. 3) Christ carefully pointed out that adultery is a concomitant of any remarriage following divorce. I would like to look at each of these three aspects of the exceptive clause in greater detail. God has some important specifics to teach us here.

One Partner, Unfaithful and Guilty

In the exceptive clause our Lord points to the guilt of only one partner. In keeping with the picture we have of God's marriage to Israel, his example presupposes that the wife is the guilty party. There is nothing in our Lord's example that would indicate that the husband is guilty. This is a point that many have great difficulty accepting. Many introduce questions into the lesson

Jesus is teaching here—questions such as, "How can he (the husband) be 100 percent innocent? Maybe he's not directly at fault, but he probably drove her to fornication somehow." It's important for us to remember that Jesus does not address himself to any extenuating circumstances. In this case one is guilty, the other innocent.

The next question that comes to mind is this: "Should this husband now divorce her for marital unfaithfulness?" The sin of fornication should never be thought of as necessitating divorce. To the contrary, even in the face of the exceptive clause we must remember that the common theme of Scripture is reconciliation—the very opposite of divorce. God ordained marriage. It was man who sinfully contrived divorce. Reconciliation is, was, and always will be God's way of dealing with sin. It should be our chief goal also. He wants all his followers to practice forgiveness, even as he demonstrated it with his bride Israel. And not only to Israel. Recall how we too were reconciled. When? "While we were still sinners . . . " (Romans 5:8).

Therefore, if genuine sorrow and heartfelt repentance follow the sin of fornication, then the Christian's duty (to God and man) is to attempt full reconciliation. In fact, fellowship with God demands forgiving one another (even in the case of marital unfaithfulness).

One can only conclude, therefore, that fornication is not a ground for divorce. At best, divorce is a gracious allowance to the innocent, given as a balm; but from the beginning divorce has not been God's solution.

But in the interest of developing the context of what our Lord is saying here, let's assume that the innocent *does* divorce the guilty wife. Two questions immediately arise: "Is she, as the guilty party, free to remarry?" "Is he, as the innocent party, free to remarry?"

In regard to remarriage, may the innocent party remarry? There are any number of Bible scholars who interpret Christ's statement to mean that whoever divorces his wife because of fornication does not commit adultery when and if he remarries. This is a paraphrase of course. One could also say that anyone who divorces his wife and marries another does not commit adultery if the divorce was sought because of marital unfaithfulness. I do not desire to defend or challenge either paraphrase. Many students of Scripture conclude that if the innocent party of a fornicated marriage divorces the guilty, unrepentant party, God will accept that divorce as permissible, complete, and final. I agree with their conclusion.

The question that immediately follows is this: "What happened to the indissolubility of marriage?" Christ said that from the beginning divorce was not the way, and Paul tells us in 1 Corinthians 7:39 that the only way a marriage is terminated is at the death of either partner. We know that we have a possible exception, but what does that really mean in regard to the indissolubility of marriage? Marriage was designed indissoluble before the fall of man and the advent of sin. Its design has not changed since the fall. *We* have changed. Marriage is still indissoluble even though man has fallen and sin has entered the picture, distorting and destroying all of God's perfect creation. Since Adam broke the perfect relationship he had with God, we also have the sinful ability to break the perfect relationship God intended for every marriage from the beginning.

Marital unfaithfulness so destroys the one-flesh union between husband and wife that God in his wisdom seems to allow relief to the innocent victim in the exceptive clause. This is a deduction, but one I make with confidence.

But what about the guilty party? May this wife remarry also? Isn't she just as divorced and free to remarry as he? Here we must be careful. Many people consider anyone who is divorced to be single and free to remarry. This misconceived notion confuses the issue, and the devil derives great pleasure from broadcasting this distorted conclusion all over television today. As Christians, we are called upon to pay close attention to the Scriptures and weed out worldly conclusions. The guilty party in a fornicated marriage is *not* free to remarry.

The best way to understand this is to think hypothetically. If the guilty party *were* free to remarry, the second marriage could not be called adulterous. But Christ said that it *would* be adultery—even for a third party (her future, second husband). "And anyone [third party] who marries a woman so divorced commits adultery" (Matthew 5:32b). But consider further: if the guilty were free to remarry, the second marriage by definition would be a holy marriage (for that is what marriage is), made possible by and through the sin of the guilty one. Does sin set us free? God rewards no one for sin. The guilty party may not remarry without committing another sin: adultery.

The Exceptive Clause—No License to Sin
The second aspect of the exceptive clause is our free will to disobey God. Christ's answer to the Pharisees began with the word "anyone." Jesus recognizes that there will be those who will divorce in spite of his command against it. But as Christians, with a free will, we are limited in our freedom to do whatever pleases God. Let me explain: Some argue that a free will has to be without constraint. But the fact is, there are conditions attached to every Christian's behavior. For instance, I may have the *freedom* to run off a cliff at full tilt without my hang glider, and I may have the *will* to glide down very slowly to the valley below, but I lack the ability to do so because of the law of gravity. It will force me downward in a manner that cancels out my *free will* to glide. It's the same with the Christian who may have the will to divorce. The force that opposes that will is his obligation

to obey the law of God. The desire to divorce is not in itself the total picture. When this desire determines one's life and spiritual consciousness, then it runs out of liberty. God's will must always take precedence over our wills. Therefore, the Christian's free will to divorce is limited by God's perfect will that we not divorce "for any and every reason" (Matthew 19:3) since "it was not this way from the beginning" (Matthew 19:8).

But because we are not able to completely escape our own will's bondage to sin, Jesus gave us directives to follow when he said that whoever divorces his wife, except for marital unfaithfulness, would have to deny his Father's will first. Our free will is not license to sin in disobedience to God's will.

Remarriage After Divorce Means Adultery
Most exception clauses are difficult to understand. This one is no different. Allow me to illustrate its complexity by using an example that does not parallel that of Matthew 19:9, but nonetheless pictures the confusion that can come from exception clauses. Suppose we had a law on the books that read, "Anyone who drives a car down the road, except he be a drunkard, and kills another person will be guilty of manslaughter." We could assume that a drunken driver in such a case would be guilty of something worse than manslaughter. But we could also assume that drunken drivers were guilty of a *lesser* charge because of the exception.

The exceptive clause in Matthew, ". . . except for marital unfaithfulness . . . ," could in itself mean a couple of different things. It could mean that marital unfaithfulness is an excuse for divorce; it could, on the other hand, mean that victims of marital unfaithfulness are (somehow!) guilty of something far *worse* than adultery. But this exceptive clause is not all we're given on the subject of divorce in Scripture. As we have seen, we learn more of the intent of the exceptive clause by comparing it with other biblical information.

We know that the Bible indicates that marriage is for life. We might then conclude that God does not intend the exceptive clause as an excuse for divorce. We also know that the Bible shows compassion toward those who are innocent and godly. We might then conclude that the exceptive clause means that victims of marital unfaithfulness are loved by God and given a solution to their agony.

However, from Christ's answer to the Pharisees recorded in Matthew 19:9 comes the warning that divorce, *for reasons other than marital unfaithfulness,* followed by another marriage constitutes adultery. Why? Why did Christ say that "anyone who divorces his wife and marries another commits adultery against her"? The only answer is that divorce is unlawful and frivolous in God's sight. The first marriage remains binding. In such a case one commits adultery *with* the second wife and *against* the first wife. Do you see how divorce is so abominable to God?

Misunderstanding the Exceptive Clause
Although the Bible clearly states that there is but one possible exception to God's command not to divorce, some nevertheless attempt to throw a smoke screen around it in hopes of obscuring its impact. A few of these attempts are more obvious than others.

There are those who attempt to enlarge upon the *scope of fornication* in an effort to broaden the limits of divorce. They argue that willful desertion might be another form of fornication simply because the marriage relationship cannot function after one has departed. Some even point to 1 Corinthians 7:15 to support their view. But since Paul was speaking of believers married to unbelievers, we cannot conclude anything as a legitimate course of action for a believer married to a fellow believer—especially not divorce! Such a position would abandon the very point God made with Israel when she willfully deserted him—reconciliation!

Then there is the age-old attempt to dilute Christ's exceptive clause by assuming that all one has to do is encourage divorce a little, and the exception will be there as a way out of the marriage. But one person cannot encourage the other to sin and not accept its consequences! One person cannot encourage his or her partner to commit fornication and then claim innocence in a divorce. God would never approve of such a divorce. Some of this careless thinking comes from the use of the terms *biblical* divorce and *biblical* grounds for divorce, as though the Bible ever approves of divorce or encourages unfaithfulness as a means of obtaining something *biblically* sound.

Then there are others who are simply bent on divorce no matter what God says about it. They are not at all interested in broadening the meaning of the word "fornication" or even looking at Scripture for any reason to divorce. They are simply determined to relieve themselves of what they consider a mismatch, one that has been a disaster from the very start. They attempt to justify themselves by statements such as, "God gave me special permission to divorce. He and I talked it out. He understands my situation." What they are actually saying is that God must have forgotten to specifically cover their unique set of circumstances in his Word.

If divorce were not so serious a sin, it would be humorous the way some employ human reason to bend Scripture to their uses. Let's look at some of these extrabiblical excuses for divorce and counter them with answers from God's Word.

SEVEN
Excuses and Replies

This chapter comes into focus because of the effects of the fall of man (Adam's original sin, after which he hid from God) and our sinful attempts to hide from God even today. The effects of sin have so distorted our horizontal (man to man) and vertical (God to man and man to God) relationships that some of us actually become convinced that we can outsmart God by outmaneuvering him on this matter of divorce.

When a Christian genuinely feels this way about his divorce and offers excuses for it apart from the one exception we've just reviewed, it might be done out of ignorance as to what God has to say about divorce, but more often it is done in confusion. It is felt that logic holds sway over God's Word. Many who have looked at Scripture do not understand God on divorce, so they react to what they consider their only problem to be— a marital difficulty.

When divorce seems to be the only solution because marital differences seem to be the only problem, then trying to lead either party toward a keener spiritual awareness is a challenge indeed. Attempts to do so are taken as artificial gestures out of step with reality and the pressures at hand. Yet, as Christian brothers and sisters we have the responsibility to witness God's truth, love, and concern to these people as well.

This chapter, then, is dedicated to the reader who has Christian friends who are not yet divorced, but who are arguing their case to both God and man in the hope of finding favor with both. In later chapters I will deal with those already divorced. But for now, let's focus on these excuses that only *seem* more immediate, and the arguments that only *seem* more logical. Here is a series of ten of the most common extrabiblical excuses for divorce.

1) "Which Is Worse: The Sin of Divorce or the Sin of Hate?"

This excuse starts out: "Which would you rather have me do—divorce my husband (or wife) and be done with it, or live with the sin of hate for the rest of my life?" A question such as this has nothing to do with what is right or wrong. Rather, it assumes wrong to be the only available choice, suggesting that you must now choose the lesser of two evils. It further implies that human logic will now become the means to arrive at the proper choice and, even worse, it assumes that this choice might please God also.

Such an unsound question, arising out of confused logic, might be exposed for what it really is by asking another wild question: "Which is worse, killing a child through an abortion or stabbing him to death at birth?" His or her reaction should be one of disgust or revolt. Immediately spot your question as an unfair one, and hand his back to him—wrapped in the same judgment.

A "lesser of two evils" question only encourages argument. Argument and contention were forbidden by Paul when he warned Timothy to withdraw from those who asked unproductive questions. He states that a person who is out of agreement with Christ is "conceited and understands nothing" (1 Timothy 6:4). Paul further warned Timothy in another letter, "Don't have anything to do with foolish and stupid arguments, because you know they produce quarrels. . . . Those who oppose him he must gently instruct, in the hope that God will grant them a repentance leading them to a knowledge of the truth, and that they will come to their senses and escape from the trap of the devil, who has taken them captive to do his will" (2 Timothy 2:23–26).

In a frightening sense, one who insists on opposing God's law on marriage (through the use of this "a lesser of two evils" question) might well be a twisted, sinful, self-centered person condemned already. God explains this possibility in his Word when he says, "Avoid foolish controversies . . . and arguments and quarrels about the law, because these are unprofitable and useless. Warn a divisive person once (Paul says), and then warn him a second time. After that, have nothing to do with him. You may be sure that such a man is warped and sinful; he is self-condemned" (Titus 3:9–11).

I chose to deal with this excuse first because it is the most common argument used and the clearest symptom of an imminent falling away from God and his grace. This tactic of asking, "Which is worse: wrong or wrong?" is the most serious mistake of any. We must pray for these people, warning them once, then again, that they might be brought back. This frail stance is no different from the unhealthy tree about which Christ told us. The tree was unable to produce good fruit because it was a corrupt tree. The same is true of this perverted question. It can only produce an unsound answer. We must hand it back as fruitless to the person asking it. Whenever it's a choice between two evils, the lesser of the two is still a corrupt selection because evil is sin!

2) "I Simply Cannot Put Up with My Partner Another Minute!"

This plea for mercy and your understanding covers a variety of discontents and may be quite persuasive. But discontent, impatience, boredom, self-will, reaching one's wits' end, or any other base excuse is not an acceptable reason for divorce, according to our Lord.

To divorce someone because you quarrel constantly with them conflicts with God's will and Word, which says that we should "live in harmony with one another; [being] sympathetic, [loving] as brothers, [being] compassionate and humble. . . . not [repaying] evil with evil or insult with insult, but with blessing, because to this you were called so that you may inherit a blessing" (1 Peter 3:8, 9). We should be quick to point out why God's blessings are not conspicuous in such a marriage.

After all, God's Word is very up-to-date here too. God once talked about Old Testament Jews who were in a hurry to find their own solutions apart from him. "Woe to obstinate children . . . to those who carry out plans that are not mine, forming an alliance, but not by my Spirit, heaping sin upon sin" (Isaiah 30:1). God also warns all New Testament believers who are living in marital difficulties and those in general dispute among themselves not to give up nor to visit the secular courts for counsel. "If any of you has a dispute with another, dare he take it before the ungodly for judgment instead of before the saints? Do you not know that God's people will judge the world? And if you are to judge the world, are you not competent to judge trivial cases? Do you not know that we will judge angels? How much more the things of this life! Therefore, if you have disputes about such matters, appoint as judges even men of little account in the church! I say this to shame you. Is it possible that there is nobody among you wise enough to judge a dispute between believers? But instead, one brother goes to law against another—and this in front of unbelievers" (1 Corinthians 6:1–6).

Therefore, when a Christian just cannot put up with his or her partner another minute—to the point of seeking relief from the courts—then that person must be reminded that if anyone throughout the history of the world ever had a *perfect* right to announce such surrender, it was our Father. He had to put up with the willful desertion, adultery, and idolatry of his bride Israel.

Now God asks us today: "What causes fights and quarrels among you? Don't they come from your desires that battle within you? You want something but don't get it. You kill and covet, but you cannot have what you want. You quarrel and fight. You do not have, because you do not ask God. When you ask, you do not receive, because you ask with wrong motives, that you may spend what you get on your pleasures. You adulterous people, don't you know that friendship with the world is hatred toward God? Anyone who chooses to be a friend of the world becomes an enemy of God" (James 4:1–4).

When a partner simply cannot put up with the marriage another minute, the solutions are not found in the divorce courts, but rather in God's Word. There we find the way to produce the fruit of his Spirit: "love, joy, peace, patience, kindness, goodness, faithfulness, gentleness and self-control. Against such things there is no law" (Galatians 5:22, 23). What a difference!

3) "Our Love for Each Other Is Gone Forever!"
Here's another common excuse: "I don't even know what love means anymore," or, "We aren't in love anymore." When someone can look you straight in the eye and tell you that he doesn't know what love means, he is unwittingly telling you that he doesn't understand the distinctiveness of Christ's *agape* love. This is why it

seems that he doesn't care if he publicly denies Christ's love.

What is it that makes Christ's love so distinctive? What makes a Christian's love unique? The answers to those questions must also come from Scripture. First of all, we know that the source of all love is God. "We love because he first loved us" (1 John 4:19). The Holy Spirit implants devotion within the Christian's heart (Romans 5:5). Christian love, therefore, is the exciting fruit of his Spirit. Christ commanded us to "love (our) neighbor as (ourselves)" (Matthew 22:39). "Love is patient, love is kind. It does not envy, it does not boast, it is not proud. It is not rude, it is not self-seeking, it is not easily angered, it keeps no record of wrongs. Love does not delight in evil but rejoices with the truth. It always protects, always trusts, always hopes, always perseveres" (1 Corinthians 13:4–7).

But if love always perseveres, how can anyone say that any couple's love is gone forever? They might imply that it was never there in the first place, and secondly, that the reason they married was a passing infatuation. If love truly does *not* exist in a marriage, obviously God isn't at the center of it. But even worse, if love is absent, God is missing from the heart of at least one of the partners, because God *is* love. "Love comes from God. Everyone who loves has been born of God and knows God. Whoever does not love does not know God, because God is love" (1 John 4:7, 8). We must remember, too, that God *commands* us to love one another—especially our mates.

It is this *agape* love, God's kind of love for us which has the capacity to forgive, that makes the Christian's marital love distinctive and indestructible. Christians should have the ability to love even when none is returned. Paul sums up this kind of love for us in these words: "Husbands, love your wives, just as Christ loved the church and gave himself up for her" (Ephesians 5:25). That's love! If love was there once, it's still there. This party must be led to see the depth of Christ's love for us before he or she is able to see the love God put there for the other partner.

4) "We Are Incompatible!"

Here's another extrabiblical excuse: "We can't get along anymore!" What does the Bible have to say about situations such as this? Two married Christians are one flesh and therefore are expected to love each other as they love themselves! God said, "After all, no one ever hated his own body" (Ephesians 5:29a). How, then, can someone be incompatible with his own flesh? Incompatibility (in the world's terminology) means a marriage is going on the rocks. The Christian's hope for what might appear to be incompatibility in marriage is based on, and found in, the Rock!

When two married believers become totally subservient to Jesus as Lord, they receive the radiance, the close communion, and the new "look" necessary for victory over any incompatibility. Is this guaranteed for everyone who can't get along anymore? Yes, it is! After all, God's way is perfect, unlike our way. His plans are everlasting and sure, inscrutable, just, and true. By following his plan for happiness in marriage we can actually eliminate the need to divorce. But instead of following God's plan for marriage, we go to men—men who only give diverse opinions. It is God who can save a marriage, not man!

Incompatibility is not a reason for a Christian to divorce; rather, it is cause for those troubled by it to seek help from the Expert on marital problems. Once again, God's practicality bursts forth. How incompatible can a Christian couple really be when they are one flesh? Our Lord tells us that "no one ever hated his own body, but he feeds and cares for it, just as Christ does the church —for we are members of his body. For this reason a man will leave his father and mother and be united to his wife, and the two will become one flesh" (Ephesians 5:29–31).

One flesh cannot be opposed to itself, whether it is the body of believers married to Christ or two Christians married into one flesh. This is why God warns us to "Get rid of all bitterness, rage and anger, brawling and slander, along with every form of malice. Be kind and compassionate to one another, forgiving each other, just as in Christ God forgave you" (Ephesians 4:31, 32). Incompatibility shows a lack of the spirituality that God gives when Christ is Lord. Divorce, for this reason too, denies Christ's lordship.

5) "God Told Me I Had an Exceptional Case."

Any student of Scripture knows that this excuse is pure malarkey! I cringe every time I hear someone say, "The Lord told me this or that . . .," unless that person follows through with a direct quotation from Scripture or a sound interpretation of a biblical truth. God has communicated through the Bible. God's immutability means that he won't change or contradict anything in Scripture through private revelations. True, his Holy Spirit will convict us of a truth and point us to Christ and his teachings, but it will always be in full agreement with what is already revealed in Scripture. God does not secretly clue us in on something out of harmony with what he has told us in Scripture. To put it another way, God does not allow extraordinary or individual marital privileges. To the contrary, he explicitly warns us that "if anyone speaks, he should do it as one speaking the very words of God" (1 Peter 4:11), and he does not violate his own command.

For our own spiritual good, we should never accept a "still small voice" that tells us something contrary to God's revealed will as recorded for us in the inspired Scriptures. There is only one possible exception to God's command not to divorce, and that's Christ's exceptive clause, just considered. He handed out no further exceptions for today's Christian.

6) "Women's Liberation Has Freed Me from the Bondage of Marriage!"

This extrabiblical excuse comes from the woman, but I have heard it from husbands as well. Usually it is the wife who says, "Everyone is equal in God's sight. I am my own person, and there is more to life than taking abuse from my chauvinistic husband while I chase dust from table to bookcase. After all, I have a responsibility toward God to be individually free so that I can realize my own potential."

Even though we might agree with some of this, for the sake of good order in society God still commands wives to be in subjection to their husbands. "Wives, submit to your husbands as unto the Lord" (Ephesians 5:22). In the bond of marriage the husband is the head of the wife, though not lord over her (Ephesians 5:23). Wives are said to be the weaker vessel (1 Peter 3:7). Yet there are those women who insist that the Bible commands us to be mutually subservient or equally submissive to one another, and they use a statement of Paul's (taken out of context) to establish a fifty-fifty relationship between themselves and their husbands. In marriage the husband is the head of the wife. When one reads all of Ephesians 5:21 through 6:5, one can see how God beautifully pictures the relationships Paul speaks of in Ephesians 5:21.

It is verse 21 that some women take out of context. It reads, "Submit to one another out of reverence for Christ." They claim that submitting to one another is mutual subjection. But this verse is only a broad principle set forth for the total body of believers (not for husbands and wives). Paul goes on to apply this principle to three particular groups of people. First, "Wives submit to your husbands as unto the Lord. For the husband is the head of the wife as Christ is the head of the church, his body, of which he is the Savior" (Ephesians 5:22). This is the first of three applications. The other two are for children and parents in Ephesians 6:1 and servants and masters in Ephesians 6:5. Therefore, when Paul states that we must submit to one another, he quickly gives us three examples: wives to husbands, children to parents, and servants to masters.

God gives us even more: "Your desire will be for your husband, and he will rule over you" (Genesis 3:16b). "Now I want you to realize that the head of every man is Christ, the head of a woman is man, and the head of Christ is God" (1 Corinthians 11:3). "Train the younger women to love their husbands and children, to be self-controlled and pure, to be busy at home, to be kind, and to be subject to their husbands, so that no one will malign the word of God" (Titus 2:4, 5). "Wives, in the same way be submissive to your husbands so that, if any of them do not believe the word, they may be won over without talk by the behavior of their wives" (1 Peter 3:1). Ponder those texts!

But God also said to the husband: "Enjoy life with your wife, whom you love" (Ecclesiastes 9:9), and "Husbands, love your wives, just as Christ loved the church and gave himself up for her to make her holy" (Ephesians 5:25). In fact, God has twice as many commands directed toward husbands, indicating that they should love and care for their wives, just as he does. Paul recognizes a divinely ordained relationship in the order of creation, and we must also. When the wife recognizes and accepts her submissiveness to her husband, she does so "as unto the Lord" (Ephesians 5:22), acknowledging his ordinance. It is clear that the biblical concept of submissiveness does not contain the notion of inferiority. Submissiveness is an act of yielding because of what is recognized as God's order of creation—his master plan for family life.

In general, those actively involved in women's liberation movements do not have this understanding of God's Word and may not use their view of the woman's role as a ground for divorce. Any who insist that their view and that of society in general is correct should be brought back to the Scriptures with a careful but complete exegesis done in patience and love.

7) "This Is The Only Way Out!"

God knows that our solutions do not always coincide with his will. His dealings are often unpopular with us and usually opposite from what our common sense seems to tell us. He knows this. After all, he said, "My thoughts are not your thoughts, neither are your ways my ways. . . . (for) as the heavens are higher than the earth, so are my ways higher than your ways and my thoughts (higher) than your thoughts" (Isaiah 55:8, 9). And the gist of his thought on divorce is this: unless it is found in Scripture don't even toy with the idea, because all that a divorce means is that at least one of you is denying the grace that I have given.

Usually the people who give this excuse honestly feel they should never have married in the first place, that their personalities were not created in such a way as to share in a marital relationship. Not every one should necessarily marry! To a degree, society is somewhat to blame here. We expect a person reaching maturity to marry. If he or she doesn't, we are puzzled and wonder what is wrong with them. Society ignores what Christ said about the single state: "(Some) have renounced marriage because of the kingdom of heaven" (Matthew 19:12b), as well as what Paul said of the widow, "In my judgment, she is happier if she stays as she is—and I think I too have the Spirit of God" (1 Corinthians 7:40). Yet, we seem to pressure each other into what society considers the normal state—marriage.

But others who claim that this is the only way out have simply stopped listening to God. They are doing a lot of praying, but little reading of Scripture. Ignorance of God's way always leads to sin. When we ignore his direction for our own direction, we become involved in sinful self-confidence that robs us of the God-confidence we so badly need in times such as these. Without trust in God, we retain darkness, ignorance, and evil in our hearts and lives. Thus in our blindness, we alienate ourselves from the very God who wants to help us. God said, "So I tell you this . . . that you must no longer live as the Gentiles do, in the futility of their thinking" (Ephesians 4:17). Ignorance of God's way is bound for failure. Usually it is at this point of confusion that one states that he or she has prayed and begged God, but now a divorce (one that God won't accept) is the only alternative left. However, when this excuse is seriously advanced, often the person stopped praying long ago. Gently warn them of this.

God knows our sinful nature and the foolish quagmires into which we get ourselves. This is why he gave us his Word as "a lamp unto [our] feet" (Psalm 119:105) to show us the path out of these traps, and even better, how to avoid them in the first place. God wants us to know that what he has joined stays joined even though we may invoke man's sham of divorce. To beg God to change his mind about divorce is a stark denial of Christ's solution. It won't work, and we should never allow someone to tell us that God exchanged his solution for theirs.

Aside from this, there are others who *demand* their solutions over God's. There is a story about such a man in the Scriptures. It's a sobering story, one that you should consider telling anyone who claims his divorce is the *only* way out. The story is told in the Old Testament but remembered by the writer of the Hebrews. "See to it that no one misses the grace of God and that no bitter root grows up to cause trouble . . . (as with) Esau, who for a single meal sold his inheritance rights as the oldest son. Afterward . . . he was rejected. He could bring about no change of mind, though he sought the blessing with tears" (Hebrews 12:15–17).

Esau sold his birthright to dissolve his immediate problem of satisfying hunger! There was no other way out, he thought. God's warning is a sobering (and often unwelcome) warning to any who feel that divorce is the only solution. Warn this person carefully, and with the power of the Holy Spirit and the Scriptures point him or her to "God's way out" instead.

8) "No Two Cases Are Alike. Mine Is Different!"
This is a trap! The symptoms may vary, but all cases *are* alike in that they all arise from a hardening or a rehardening of the heart. That is to say, they have a spiritual problem. That is why I maintain that the basic *cause* for all divorce is the same for everyone. It is a lack of spiritual fervor.

All cases are alike in that both the Christian and the non-Christian sin in divorcing. Each will have to pay a penalty, but the fine will be dissimilar. One standard of obedience applies to all men, but all men are not held equally accountable. Jesus illustrated this fact in these words: "That servant who knows his master's will and does not get ready or does not do what his master wants will be beaten with many blows. But the one who does not know and does things deserving punishment will be beaten with few blows" (Luke 12:47, 48a). So those denominations who argue, "No two cases are alike. . . ." are only partly correct. This fact, however, does not dismiss the biblical truth that every divorce will be judged negatively by God, even though to varying degrees.

Denominations that refer the issue of divorce to their local churches probably do so believing that "No two cases are alike." What they don't address themselves to is the obligation (that all Christians share) to judge all divorce as contrary to God's revealed will. In this respect, too, all cases are alike.

9) "Our Marriage Certainly Wasn't Made in Heaven!"
There are many who will seriously try to explain, "God never joined us, our marriage was never intended to be, it was not God's will in the first place." Statements such as these are not an uncommon rejoinder to the verse, "What God has joined together, let man not separate" (Matthew 19:6). "God never joined us," they reply!

If this were true, this person would be condemning himself rather than freeing himself. If God never joined them, then no one else did either. Marriage is an institution of God, not man. If they were never joined by God, then their confession is adultery; and if there are children involved, they are illegitimate. If two Christians are married, they were married by God. Think about that for a moment. Marriage is God's divine institution, not man's invention; and God-ordained marriage is to last a lifetime.

This excuse is no argument at all and surely not a reason for divorce. It is only a man-made apology. For the believer witnessing to this situation, the apology must be recognized as a desperate attempt at human rationalization in order to avoid Scripture's condemnation of divorce. Simply remind this person that God hates divorce.

10) *Other Excuses*

A great variety of excuses exist for disobeying God through divorce—too many to list separately. Often they are not offered separately but in clusters, as parts of heart-rending, true-life stories. Here is an example of one such story. As you read on, you may be tempted to say, "I heard that one the other day!"

It might sound something like this: "The man I married loved me once and I loved him, but all that is gone now. Today, our marriage is full of bitterness, hate, envy, and strife. Everything that was beautiful has disappeared. The responsibilities once shared exist no longer. Our children pit us against each other in arguments, and no one can win that way. We are totally unsuited for each other, and I suffer mental cruelty. He makes unbiblical demands of me, and he is very jealous—something he never used to be. When I married him, I thought he would become a Christian. He said he would, but he didn't. Now he won't go to church. He won't search for a job and can't hold on to one when someone gives him work. He's selfish, proud, and negligent. I have to be both mother and father to the kids. Lately, we don't talk, we only shout. More than once, I have been physically beaten by him. He will pout for weeks at a time and then whines when I complain about it. Our sex life is dead, and he only uses me to satisfy his animal instincts. We're in debt over our heads, and now he's started drinking a lot more than he used to. I think he picks up companionship in the bars. He's really never matured, and when he feels like it, he will just take off for days at a time and never tell me where he's going or been; he says it's none of my business. Now it's finished, washed up, done forever, and I'm glad because there is no marriage to save. It's been dead for years, but we've just been covering it up for the sake of the kids. Feelings of love are nonexistent; in fact, if there is any emotion left, it's pure hatred! I am convinced that our marriage was never part of God's plan because God never intended me, or anyone else, to have to suffer like this for a lifetime. I want out, and I want out *now!* Anyway, God understands me, and I've settled this matter between him and me. It's none of anyone's business!"

Now let's add a few twists to the story: Suppose this woman also said, "Without this marital burden, I could be a better Christian. I could pray better, enjoy going to church again, actually worship God, spend more time in the Word, join a solid Bible study group, and even witness my faith more effectively without this burden pulling me down constantly." That would convince many Christians. And with Christian people agreeing with something like this, it's easy for the confused victim to assume that God approves also.

We don't dispute all that she said. Surely she could accomplish much more without the pressures of a deteriorating marriage eating away at her spiritual life. Granted, peace and tranquility are conducive to improving one's spiritual awareness. We cannot argue with her desired result; but we must take issue with her method of attaining it. It's opposed to God's way! Nor may we argue with her statement that God never intended a marriage to come to this; he didn't! But listening to our own common sense, or that of our well-meaning friends, is not heeding God. Fabricated answers, especially those that are well-rationalized, may sound great at the moment, but they only reflect the thoughts of man and not the wishes and commands of God. The point is that we do not have the right to use God's perfect goals as excuses to divorce. Doing so cuts God right out of his own solution—the fullness of his Spirit.

The important thing to remember here is that God knows our heart and the problem. He also knows well the desperation associated with a troubled marriage. Now he wants us to understand and apply his solution, whether it's for a marital problem, a prior divorce, or a second marriage following a sinful divorce. If we do it our way instead, we are running ahead, without God. The Bible warns us of certain failure when we take matters into our own hands.

In pointing out Scripture to those in marital trouble, we shouldn't condemn one for wishing that evil forces be removed from their lives. Nor should we talk down, or misrepresent in any way, the advantages of a happier life. The difficulty in answering such a person lies in demonstrating conclusively to him or her that the solution does not consist of getting rid of someone. Rather, it requires grabbing hold of Someone mightier than ourselves. The troublesome backsliding, deserting, irrational, and irritating partner shouldn't be eliminated; the *cause* should be eradicated instead. We are not really dealing with a person, as such, but the *evil* that controls that person. Paul touched on this very point when he said, "For our struggle is not against flesh and blood, but against the rulers, against the authorities, against the powers of this dark world and against the spiritual forces of evil in the heavenly realms" (Ephesians 6:12).

The visible flesh-and-blood partner is not the basic problem! The real problem is the spiritual barrenness that gives way to the work of the devil. Jesus Christ is victor over sin and the devil. As Lord of our lives, he is our defense, our hiding place, our fortress, our refuge, and even our shield against everything that a failing partner could be or do. With Christ as Lord, we are *more* than conquerors because "we know that in all things God works for the good of those who love him, who have been called according to his purpose" (Romans 8:28).

When someone is plagued with marital symptoms that could lead to divorce, it may be difficult to help him or her understand that, as Christians, we are more than conquerors when we must continue to live with an offending party. Let God be the one to demonstrate how this works. Take the party involved through the Romans 8:28–39 passage very slowly. It reads:

> *We know that in all things God works for the good of those who love him, who have been called according to his purpose. For those God foreknew he also predestined to be conformed to the likeness of his Son, that he might be the firstborn among many brothers. And those he predestined, he also called; those he called, he also justified; those he justified, he also glorified. What, then, shall we say in response to this? If God is for us, who can be against us? He who did not spare his own Son, but gave him up for us all—how will he not also, along with him, graciously give us all things? Who will bring any charge against those whom God has chosen? It is God who justifies. Who is he that condemns? Christ Jesus, who died—more than that, who was raised to life—is at the right hand of God and is also interceding for us. Who shall separate us from the love of Christ? Shall trouble or hardship or persecution or famine or nakedness or danger or sword? As it is written: "For your sake we face death all day long; we are considered as sheep to be slaughtered." No, in all these things we are more than conquerors through him who loved us. For I am convinced that neither death nor life, neither angels nor demons, neither the present nor the future, nor any powers, neither height nor depth, nor anything else in all creation, will be able to separate us from the love of God that is in Christ Jesus our Lord.*

From this text we see that staying with a troublesome partner is not the same as accepting the evil forces behind the trouble. Yet the reader may ask, How are we more than conquerors?

In the first place, we will not only win, but we will do so without ever losing a marriage! Even more, we will be gaining the soul of the feuding and offending partner.

Thus, we win with glory and honor and with peace. It can only happen in the power and love of Jesus' Spirit; never through our own strength, rationalization, or wishful thinking. Naturally, the person complaining is at wits' end. He or she is fighting a strong and invisible foe—the devil. But if we give up in the middle of the battle, we give up on God. This would be foolish! We are not losers, nor merely conquerors; we are *more* than conquerors.

In summary, there are probably many unbiblical excuses for divorce other than what I have given. Just the other day I heard a man who was having an affair give a new excuse: "I didn't go out looking for another woman, she just came by . . . it just happened!" The person hearing that excuse looked him straight in the eye and said, "Adam didn't look for the forbidden fruit, nor pick it; Eve just happened along and he took a bite!" That was enough to say. The excuse fell limp. I have great confidence in the Spirit's ability to bring the proper words to bear in situations where we find ourselves up against a new excuse. God is never wrong; so all we must do is tell them what God has taught us!

EIGHT
Divorce and the Church

The role of the church in a divorce case is about as popular with those involved as the role of the dentist to someone with a cavity! Both church and dentist are considered necessary evils, yet each desires to treat the real cause behind the pain, not merely mask it.

Because the role of the church in disciplinary matters is odious to most people, numerous questions about church discipline remain unanswered. Questions such as, "Why should some stuffed-shirt office bearer from the church have to involve himself in my personal affairs?" obviously demonstrate a lack of appreciation for the true *intent* behind the intrusion. What is that intent? Well, it can be summed up in one word: *love.*

Church discipline is divine love; that is, God's concern for those hurting the most. It comes in the form of a firm warning to break away from the influence of sin and the devil. Church discipline is divine discipline since the organized Church of Jesus Christ was and is called by God himself, thus divinely instituted. Further, the head of the Church is Jesus Christ himself. Therefore, it is our Lord who does the disciplining, through fellow believers at the outset and later through the church officers if the initial admonition is not heeded. Scripture emphatically states that the Church is the living body of our Lord (Ephesians 1:22, 23).

Yet, those receiving discipline always seem to discredit it as something unnecessary and, in their case, certainly unfair. They forget that each member must *submit* to, not merely accept, the discipline of the Church by virtue of his or her faith in God and his Holy Word. Let's not forget that Christ firmly instructs the church elders to keep the church pure! "Those who sin are to be rebuked publicly, so that the others may take warning" (1 Timothy 5:20), which means that as members of his body, every church member is obligated to follow his commands. This includes the one which explicitly prohibits two Christians from divorcing. When they refuse to follow God's command, the church is to publicly rebuke them.

The church is forced to play a disciplinary role with members who seek a divorce since no believer has a personal or private life apart from Jesus Christ (the head of the Church). Each of us is adopted by grace into God's larger family (Romans 8:15). And as sons of God, we relinquish all power over our own lives. Therefore, the role of the church is obligatory in cases where one of its members begins to look for solutions apart from Christ. God divinely authorizes church leaders to care for each member (Hebrews 13:17). Their spiritual disciplining need not demand a full marital reconciliation at the outset, but would be (by the very nature of marital discipline) the first step toward that goal.

Perhaps the greatest complication surrounding church discipline is the fact that the church is not advised early enough of marital symptoms. It's not until these become full-blown spiritual problems that they become detected. At this point, many misconstrue the solution to be full reconciliation. But this cannot be done in the presence of the spiritual problem that caused the symptom to appear in the first place. We must deal gently with the underlying spiritual problem before we mention reconciliation. Reconciliation is a natural conclusion to spiritual rejuvenation. We must treat the cause. By doing so, the effect will disappear automatically.

For our purposes in this chapter, I assume that the church is officially notified very late in the marital discord; that is, after a separation is already effected or a civil divorce proceeding already has begun. I want us to treat the *problem* in its most difficult setting. I want the reader to bear in mind that what is now said about the church's role also applies to all of the earlier stages of marital disharmony as well.

The Role of the Church with Separated Christians

Usually by the time a church is reliably notified of a separation it has already become public knowledge. The couple's announcement may be intended to serve notice to the church that something far worse is about to happen very soon! Yet the couple's very act of informing the church seems to create some hope within a membership that they seek God's solution. The announcement to the church may mean that this couple has decided that divorce actually *does* deny Christ's lordship, so they are merely announcing a separation until they can sort out the basic spiritual problem.

Thus we have two possibilities—first, those who inform the church because they are sure that something worse is about to happen—namely, a divorce outside of Scripture's guidelines; and second, those who separate until they can rededicate themselves to Christ and each other. Either way, each couple is confessing that they have not as yet found a God-directed path out of their mess at home, and this should be the only message the church hears. In each case the couple is demonstrating an acute spiritual problem, and in both cases they've called it a marital problem.

Now, how does the church deal with these situations? In neither case should the church pounce on them for having a spiritual problem, nor condemn them for having waited too long. To do so could turn them away and would be a more serious mistake than the one of which the disciples were guilty when they unthinkingly shooed the little children away from our Lord. The role of the church must always reflect the mind, love, and patience of Christ. After all, he came not to condemn, but to save.

It is difficult for church leaders (or anyone else in tune with the Scriptures) to hear of a sin without condemning it. We forget that the persons involved no doubt condemned it themselves after they fell into it. For those seeking help, the sin is already a fact of life, not something to be debated and condemned. For the persons separated (or for one having initiated civil divorce proceedings), the role of the church must be to prevent the persons involved from further denying or rejecting God, his Word, his Son, and their marriage.

Even knowing all this, there are many church officials who begin speaking to the surface issues of divorce by piously quoting Scripture that prohibits long separations or divorce instead of dealing with the spiritual illness that is causing the symptom to appear. Talking down divorce may be talking up a scriptural position, but at this point (with a couple willing to listen to solutions), it seems senseless to condemn. It only adds to the frustration already present. A speech full of "thou shalt nots" could easily panic one or both toward the only escape they recognize. They might be understandably tempted to say, "No one understands anyway, so why stick around to work it out? Let's just finish it off with a divorce, come what may, and get it over with!"

For the church to go to the opposite extreme by suggesting that they go home and pray about their symptoms is to ignore the probability that they have already attempted this. These are spiritually sick people! Couples in this fix are at their wits' end and suffer from a lot more than a pressing marital misunderstanding. Even as spiritually hurting Christians, they no doubt experience inner feelings of guilt already, knowing in their hearts that their actions betray the very Christ they profess to follow. The church has to be sensitive enough to center its consideration on the problem (a spiritual and personal relationship to Jesus Christ) and not drift off into the more obvious symptoms of divorce and separation.

Specifically how should the church conduct such a meeting? I can only suggest a way that I believe appropriate. I think it is vital that a dialogue be established and this can best be done by asking them some questions—questions to which they *can* still answer yes. Questions such as these: "Do you still believe in God?" "Do you still consider the Bible to be God's Holy Word?" "Do you believe the Bible is relevant today and is meaningful for correction, reproof, and teaching?" "Do you know in your hearts that God was thoughtful and complete in his Word and included *everything* we must know in order to live and die happily?" And then, perhaps the most important question of all, one designed to establish a common ground, "Do you accept the fact that but for the grace of God any one of us present would be in the same situation in which you find yourselves?"

We now have common ground and ground rules. The ground rule is that for all future discussion the holy Word of God is the established criterion. From this point we may open it and read it together. But where do we start? I can suggest where *not* to start. I do not think it advisable to begin with any of the passages I have been quoting throughout this book that speak of marriage or divorce. I would rather begin with a passage that would establish more common ground to stand on together. Such a passage might possibly be Romans 7:21–25 which reads: "When I want to do good, evil is right there with me. For in my inner being I delight in God's law. But I see another law at work in the members of my body, waging war against the law of my mind and making me a prisoner of the law of sin at work within my members. What a wretched man I am!" Stop right there and agree that every Christian has this battle raging within him. Let them know that they are normal. Continually seek common ground without compromising yourselves, the church, or God's Word or will. Finally come to the rest of the text: "Who will rescue me from this body of death? Thanks be to God—through Jesus Christ our Lord." There's the solution: Jesus Christ *as* Lord!

There are many other texts one could turn to in Bible study. I would suggest spending the entire session reviewing texts that point to our propensity to sin. Let them ponder this one fact: They came thinking they would be condemned harshly, but instead the elders talked about God and his love; how easy it is to sin, but God supplies a way out of every temptation.

However, if they refuse the advice, love, and concern of Christ provided them through the eldership of the church, if they continue in their state of marital discord or prolonged separation, or if they actually seek a civil divorce, *then* they must be placed under the discipline of the church without delay. This is the obligation of the elders of the church, based on Scripture's own directives: "Those who sin are to be rebuked publicly, so that the others may take warning. I charge you, in the sight of God and Christ Jesus and the elect angels, to keep these instructions without partiality, and to do nothing out of favoritism" (1 Timothy 5:20, 21).

There are two aspects to church discipline: redemption and punishment. The former is evangelistic in nature and seeks to restore the sinner, while the latter is punitive and involves cutting off dead branches. It is the final step of church discipline. Perhaps a more accurate way of looking at any church discipline is that it is discipleship intended to teach and train as well as correct or punish. All church discipline is God-directed, but too often it is misconstrued *only* as an immediate punitive act designed on the part of the elders to kick someone out of the church. This is surely not the intent. Yet, how can hard feelings be avoided when one person must point out the fault in another, unless we carefully establish that except for the grace of God any one of the elders or congregation would be in the same position.

God promises to bless when we are obedient and to punish when we are disobedient. In his love, he warns the disobedient, unrepentant, and hardened of heart that he will blot their names out of the book of life (Psalm 69:28), cast them out as fit for nothing (Matthew 5:13), and disown them before the Father (2 Timothy 2:12) if they continue to disobey. He promises forgiveness to the disobedient only in the face of true, sincere, and complete repentance. Therefore, the purpose of all church discipline is to lead one back to spiritual health—restoration.

But if the overall purpose of church discipline is to restore one spiritually, and if it is God-directed to accomplish this goal, then why is it so often "unsuccessful"? Part of the answer lies in the fact that there is a tendency "not to forget" on the part of the rest of us in the church. This makes "successful" chastisement very difficult. Too many of us remember the bad in someone else instead of remembering that, but for the grace of God, we'd be the recipient of the discipline ourselves. We fail to see the grace and joy that God pours out from heaven to those who have sinned and repented. Instead, we remember the failures. Look at the jubilant hoopla the prodigal son received. Why? Because he sinned? No! Because he sinned, recognized his sin, confessed it, repented from it, and *returned.*

Sometimes God crowns our foolish mistakes with a

degree of learning that is unobtainable in the church pew. Grace abounds for every repentant sinner, and when a couple rediscovers their marriage, church people should allow God's grace to shine through and not harp on the failure that brought it about. "We know that in all things God works for the good of those who love him, who have been called according to his purpose" (Romans 8:28).

Certainly it is difficult to admit wrong! It is natural for us to justify our mistakes in order to look better. It is natural for people to reject discipline or chastisement. The seed of rebellion is ever-present. This rebellion may take the form of transferring church membership from the disciplining church to another or permanently resigning from the church before becoming disassociated or excommunicated. This sort of action on the part of the sinner does not change matters where God is concerned, nor does it change God's mind about the necessity to confess the sin and repent.

But, thank God, there are couples who *do* accept Christ's softening touch through church discipline and *do* sincerely repent from their purpose to sin. They end the separation or lay aside the plan to divorce, and they return to each other with a new hope, new faith, and a new start.

How Do We Recognize Sincere Repentance?
We are at a point now where we must consider what constitutes true repentance. Sometimes, as in the case of one who has already divorced and remarried, repentance is hard to detect. Such a person is limited as to what corrective, remorseful action he or she can take. A clear understanding of exactly what makes up godly sorrow for sin is essential to every point that follows:

First, let's look at the Word of God to find our definition of true repentance:

"Hear the word I speak and give them warning from me. . . . say to your countrymen, 'The righteousness of the righteous man will not save him when he disobeys, and the wickedness of the wicked man will not cause him to fall when he turns from it. The righteous man, if he sins, will not be allowed to live because of his former righteousness.' If I tell the righteous man that he will surely live, but then he trusts in his righteousness and does evil, none of the righteous things he has done will be remembered; he will die for the evil he has done. And if I say to the wicked man, 'You will surely die,' but he then turns away from his sin and does what is just and right—if he gives back what he took in pledge for a loan, returns what he has stolen, follows the decrees that give life, and does not evil, he will surely live; he will not die. None of the sins he has committed will be remembered against him. He has done what is just and right; he will surely live. Yet your countrymen say, 'The way of the Lord is not just.' But it is their way that is not just. If a righteous man turns from his righteousness and does evil, he will die for it. And if a wicked man turns away from his wickedness and does what is just and right, he will live by doing so. Yet, O house of Israel, you say, 'The way of the Lord is not just.' But I will judge each of you according to his own ways"(Ezekiel 33:7, 12–20).

This text shows us, among other things, that sincere repentance is a *public deed:* giving back what was taken, returning what was stolen, living a right life pleasing to God, and doing no more evil. Our deeds are so important to God and so much a part of true repentance that God mentions them again in the New Testament: "Prove [your] repentance by [your] deeds" (Acts 26:20). In the case of a Christian who has divorced but is not yet remarried, he or she can prove repentance through reconciliation (the theme of all Scripture) and thereby *give back* to the other partner (and to the children, if there are children involved) a reunited, Christ-centered, Christ-honoring home. This deed would be one visible proof of repentance. (Immediately the question comes to mind: "Must a remarried divorcee then undo the second marriage?" We will deal with matters concerning the remarried divorcee in the following chapter.)

Attitudes are also a part of sincere repentance. Read what God records about *proper attitudes.* The Israelites demonstrated proper attitudes toward God when he pointed out their sin to them. "The Israelites said to the Lord, 'We have sinned. Do with us whatever you think best, but please rescue us now'" (Judges 10:15). Take note of their attitude of complete surrender to God's authority. "Do with us whatever you think best," they said. They openly displayed an attitude of truthfulness with God: "We have sinned. . . ." They did not attempt to rationalize their sin, nor cover it up, nor blame anyone else; they simply admitted to God that they had indeed sinned.

So public deeds and proper attitudes are important components of the sinner's sincere repentance, but there is more. What *kind* of attitudes are essential to prove true repentance? *Regret* is one. God outlines true regret for us in Isaiah 22:12:

> *The Lord, the Lord Almighty, called you on that day to weep and to wail, to tear out your hair and put on sackcloth.*

And in Joel 2:12, 13 God tells us more about the fact that sincere repentance includes absolute regret:

> *"Return to me with all your heart, with fasting and weeping and mourning. Rend your heart and not your garments."*

Regret (or godly sorrow) cannot be only an emotional or superficial manifestation. We must therefore be careful not to place too much weight on obvious or shallow emotions while judging a person's repentance. A sincerely repentant person will absolutely regret a given sin and wish it had never happened, not because he or she was found out, nor because of the effects and consequences of the sin, but because it *wronged* Almighty God! Regret must always be separate from any fear of punishment or loss of one's own reputation.

Besides the attitude of absolute regret, true repentance must also contain a genuine *hatred for the sin* committed. God tells us this in Ezekiel 35:5, 6 where he says, " 'Because you (Edom) harbored an ancient hostility and delivered the Israelites over to the sword at the time of their calamity . . . therefore as surely as I live . . . I will give you over to bloodshed and it will pursue you. Since you did not hate bloodshed, bloodshed will pursue you.' " Repentance should include a willingness and eagerness to speak out publicly against the sin as a warning to others to avoid it; thus once again we see repentance by deeds.

Add yet another element: *humility*. God warns us in Matthew 3:8, 9: "Produce fruit in keeping with repentance. And do not think you can say to yourselves, 'We have Abraham as our Father.' I tell you that out of these stones God can raise up children for Abraham." Reliance upon our heritage, or good works, or any promise of God prior to the sin is only false security and an evidence of a lack of humility which God requires from every repentant person who comes before his throne of grace to ask for forgiveness. We may not rely on a lifelong track record of obedience prior to a sin that we now refuse to confess because of pride.

There is yet another vital aspect to a sincerely repentant attitude: *turning away from the sin and turning to God.*

Turning away from sin is nothing short of conversion from the sin. God demands as evidence of our broken spirit and our broken and contrite heart a new life, a conversion, a turning away from sin, and a turning back to him. This is also called a *change of mind* about the sin itself. The truly repentant person demonstrates that he or she has a changed (new) mind about the sin.

There is still another ingredient of sincere repentance: *total disregard for one's own self.* Look at how David blamed no one else, only himself, for his sin:

> *Have mercy on me, O God . . . blot out my transgressions. Wash away all my iniquity and cleanse me from my sin. For I know my transgressions, and my sin is always before me. Against you, you only, have I sinned and done what is evil in your sight, so that you are proved right when you speak and justified when you judge. Surely I have been a sinner from birth, sinful from the time my mother conceived me* (Psalm 51:1–5).

We must remember two things: first, any sin can be forgiven (Ephesians 1:7); and second, the forgiven sin should not then ever be willfully repeated (Hebrews 10:-26).

The secret to true and sincere repentance is the Holy Spirit working in the heart of the sinner and the willingness of the sinner to heed his workings. But the facts of life are these: Most Christians suffering from marital disharmony are so spiritually ill that they refuse to repent or be treated for the underlying spiritual problem. Many prefer to go right ahead and obtain a civil divorce against God's will, despite the efforts of the church. By ignoring the warnings concerning their lack of repentance or the fact that they now intend to add sin to sin, they thereby move themselves closer to disassociation or excommunication from the church.

Divorced People Who Desire Church Membership

Divorced Christians fall into two separate categories: those divorced before becoming Christian and those divorced since becoming Christian. There is a vast difference between the two situations, and we must carefully distinguish between them. Those divorced prior to accepting Christ *do not retain the sin of divorce after their conversion.* Why is a new Christian who was divorced before his or her conversion able to become a member of the church in good standing, while a Christian who gets a divorce after conversion is placed under discipline and accused of sinning?

First of all, the sin is not the same. The Christian knew better and had the grace (in Christ) to make his or her marriage work, whereas the convert did not have the power of Christ in his or her heart at the time of the divorce. The new Christian lost his or her old self in Jesus, and all previous sin was thereby rendered powerless. Paul declares, "Therefore if anyone is in Christ, he is a new creation; the old has gone, the new has come" (2 Corinthians 5:17). The old has not only left, but has become non-existent, and therefore it is powerless to convict. Paul again details this for us with these words: "For we know that our old self was crucified with him so that the body of sin might be rendered powerless, that we should no longer be slaves to sin—because anyone who has died has been freed from sin. . . . The death he died, he died to sin once for all; but the life he lives, he lives to God" (Romans 6:6, 7, 10). God's peace, mercy, and glory fulfilled the debt of the law through Jesus Christ, thus eradicating the past in the new convert.

Paul gives us another reason why the new Christian may be considered free of all old sins: "The old has gone, the new has come! All this is from God, who reconciled us to himself through Jesus Christ and gave us the ministry of reconciliation" (2 Corinthians 5:17b, 18). Paul is saying here that God fully reconciles believers to himself when they accept Jesus, and then he gives them the ministry of reconciling *others*. That, in a nutshell, is how the church (made up of forgiven sinners) is to accept the divorcee who has become converted since his or her divorce and wishes to become a member of the church. Welcome him or her with joy!

Someone is sure to be wondering, "Is the forgiveness God grants the unbeliever who divorced different from what God offers the believer who divorced?" The answer is no. In both cases the forgiveness is completely the same, but the parties receiving it differ. The believer, being married to Jesus Christ, had to deny Christ's lordship since he was *one* with Christ, not separate from Christ as was the unbeliever. The believer was included in the citizenship of believers, not a foreigner to the covenants and promises. The believer possessed hope in God, whereas the unbeliever was without hope. Finally, the believer had the Way, the way to make a marriage work.

We can only conclude that for the Christian a divorce is a greater sin since it also represented a rehardening of the redeemed heart. This is very offensive to God because Jesus had already destroyed the sin barrier between the believer and God, thus giving access to the Father through Christ and making the Christian one with Christ. The Christian tossed all this aside when he disobediently divorced.

Forgiveness Does Not Include a Right to Remarry
It must be reemphasized that through all of this neither the mature Christian nor the new convert possesses a right to remarry. This is even true in the light of the forgiveness they have received. God's forgiveness eradicates the sin of denying his lordship, but not necessarily the consequences of the sin. Specifically, forgiveness does not make the unrecognized divorce a recognized

divorce. Let me illustrate with an example. Picture a child who has thrown a stone through someone's window. He can be sorry for it, confess it, and be forgiven, even be exempted from paying for the broken window; but none of this *mends* the window. The point is that forgiveness does not necessarily eradicate the consequences of the sin. Being forgiven for a divorce does not make one single. There was no God-recognized divorce in the first place. It is the denial of Christ's lordship that must be forgiven—the denial that attempted to accomplish a fruitless effort to dissolve an indissoluble marriage. To consider that a person (forgiven for trying the impossible) is thereby *granted* the impossible is absurd. Forgiveness for the sin of divorce does not free one to remarry; instead it allows one to demonstrate a Christlike forgiveness to his or her partner and become reconciled.

Resisting a Divorce Does Not Grant a Right to Remarry
The next question that comes to mind is, "What about the person who didn't want the divorce and even fought it all the way? What's his or her position with the church, and may he or she remarry?" This question comes up repeatedly as though there might be some virtue in not specifically wanting to be a part of the sin that involves both parties. Contesting the divorce does not grant permission to remarry. Christ said that if there was no marital unfaithfulness, there was no divorce. Therefore, neither party may remarry; not seeking the divorce makes absolutely no difference as far as remarriage is concerned. Jesus makes this point exceptionally clear by bringing into his illustration a third party who also had no fault in the divorce. He said, "Anyone who divorces his wife . . . causes her to commit adultery, and anyone [third party] who marries a woman so divorced commits adultery" (Matthew 5:32). Surely if the third party (who

107

also had nothing to do with causing the divorce or marital discord) would be guilty of adultery, then surely the person who didn't want the divorce and fought it all the way would be just as guilty of adultery upon remarriage.

Therefore, regardless of the forgiveness received or the fact that one may have contested the unrecognized divorce, remarriage is forbidden. It is the duty of the church to tenderly instruct its members according to Scripture's teachings. Anything short of reconciliation is a refusal to truly repent.

NINE
The Divorced, Remarried Christian

As we begin to consider the toughest theological aspect of this mixed, twisted situation, we are immediately faced with a wide range of opinions from Bible scholars as well as sentiments from those who have graduated from the school of experience.

All claim to have solutions. Some demand that the remarried divorcee leave the second marriage and return to the first (or at least leave the second partner). Others advocate the kind of twentieth-century permissiveness that allows anything that feels good. So, what is the true and right thing to do?

Have you ever wearied over the search for God's righteous solution to this combination of problems and symptoms? Surely God knew the unimaginable mess into which some of us would fall. Isn't it reasonable then that the proper solution will only be found in his Word? However, God's solution is not didactically or explicitly given anywhere in Scripture, so it will have to come from a total, comprehensive picture of the Scripture's message. These understandings of God's Word might oppose some of our favorite deductions, those we have adopted over the years. But this may be a good thing.

Our thoughts are not like his thoughts, and our ways are not like his ways. If they were, we wouldn't have this problem.

As I stated previously, divorce itself is not an unforgivable sin when followed by sincere repentance. But would we say that the sin of the remarried divorcee *is* unforgivable? How can this series of complicated sins, with their sinful, lasting, and entangled consequences, be forgiven? In other words, is the adultery of which Christ spoke a "continual" adultery? If it is, and if the solution were to stop sinning, wouldn't a second divorce also be contrary to God's will and Word and therefore be another sin? Can we ever rid ourselves of a given sin by sinning once more?

It's on this matter of "continual" adultery and the question of how God could forgive a person who had disobediently divorced and then sinfully remarried that there seems to be the greatest debate.

The reader may have picked up my feeling about this already. I believe the adultery in a second marriage *is* continual, but I must quickly add a qualification. I believe that it is continual *until* one of three things happen: first, until either the remaining party invokes the exceptive clause (I will explain this later); second, until the death of one of the original partners dissolves the earlier marriage; or third, until confession and sincere repentance followed by divine forgiveness dissolves the sin involved (I will explain this later also).

Those who oppose the view of "continual" adultery attempt to do away with it in four interesting ways: first, they say that all married persons are not (or were not) necessarily married by God; second, that a remarried divorcee is not actually married in the second marriage; third, that a second marriage automatically dissolves the first marriage; and fourth, that the only solution to "continual" adultery in a divorce-remarriage is another divorce or separation. Since any conclusion will have to be based on God's Word and the correct application of it, let me first deal with these four *false* notions which only cloud the issue.

1) *"Not All Married Couples Are Married in God's Sight"*

Those who argue this point hold that in the case of a divorcee who has remarried, the *original* marriage wasn't necessarily recognized by God. These people might assert that such a marriage doesn't really count and that the subsequent marriage, then, is legitimate.

But it is God who holds the keys to his institution of marriage! Marriage is God's holy ordained formula, not man's invention. Therefore, because God holds the rights to marriage, it is only through his common grace that any marriage is instituted. That is why we read, "What God has joined . . ."

2) *"Remarried Divorcees Are Not Actually Married a Second Time"*

This argument holds that a remarried divorcee is not actually married *again* in God's sight since the first marriage was (and is) indissoluble as long as the original partner is alive. While I agree marriages are indissoluble, I disagree that a remarried divorcee isn't remarried in God's sight. He or she is very much married. As a matter of fact, he or she is married *to two people at once* and commits "continual" adultery. Christ said in Matthew 19:9, "I tell you that anyone who divorces his wife . . . *and marries another woman* commits adultery." Therefore the remarried divorcee is married twice and a polygamist! If marriages are for life, and if a divorced person (not then divorced in God's sight at all) marries another, that person is twice married. That's what makes the sin the sin of adultery.

3) "There Is No Continual Adultery
Because the Second Marriage Dissolved the First"
The third false concept, that all second marriages spon-
taneously dissolve the first, is also without biblical warrant. Divorce is an ineffective contrivance of man used
in an unsuccessful attempt to destroy the permanency of
what God had established as an *irrevocable trust* for life.
Therefore, if the first marriage is not dissolved by the
divorce (because it lacked biblical support), then how
could a remarriage do anything but add sin to sin? To
put it another way, the first sin of divorce had no authoritative power to undo God's indissoluble work of joining
two as one. How could a second sin (that of a second
marriage) accomplish anything the first sin failed to do?
Sins add up, they don't subtract—in fact, one could
argue that in this case they multiply! Any divorce (except it be the case of fornication) is meaningless in its
effect on the permanency of a marriage. Any second
marriage is likewise meaningless in dissolving the first.

However, there is an exception here. If someone who
gets a divorce marries again, he or she commits adultery.
This does not *break* the first marriage nor dissolve it, but
it gives a right to the remaining party to exercise the
exceptive clause and be freed from the first marriage.
Some readers will immediately ask the question, "How
is someone supposed to exercise the exceptive clause at
this late date after the divorce is already history?" Well,
the divorce is only "history" as far as the state is concerned, not where God is concerned. The way the exceptive clause is exercised at this point is through the *remarriage* of the *remaining* party, as outlined in Matthew 5:32
and 19:9. While this is proper for the remaining party
(because of the adultery associated with the remarriage
of the first party), it is *never* right for the first party,
regardless of whether it is the man or the woman. Why?
Simply because before either remarried, neither had the
right to remarry. After the first party breaks marital

faithfulness (by remarrying), the *remaining* party can claim the exceptive clause and publicly certify the destruction of the original marriage by publicly remarrying.

This is precisely where all the confusion comes in. You see, God's permission to seek relief is only offered the sexually *offended* party, never the sexually *offending* party. This God-given exception remains the sole biblical prerogative of the party that remained faithful. The exceptive clause is not applicable to the guilty in, by, or through the act of sinning. There is a great deal of difference between the *offended* person being able to dissolve the *effects of the offense* (by claiming what can be understood to be a God-given right to divorce) and the *offender* having authority to dissolve a marriage.

4) "The Solution to the Divorce-Remarriage Trap Is Another Divorce"

Those who advocate a second divorce to cure the problem of "continual" adultery forget that a second divorce is as meaningless as the first. The offender may never claim his or her offense as a reason for another divorce. Sin does not cancel sin!

Another way to look at it is this: since the sin of the first divorce (which was only a civil court action) did not break the original marriage as far as God is concerned, how could the sin of a second divorce do anything more?

This fourth false notion, compelling the remarried to divorce again, might sincerely be based on the idea that divorce eradicates the consequences of the previous sin (remarriage) and that our Lord's forgiveness is based upon such an eradication of sin. This is a fallacy. Bear in mind that there are two requirements for reconciliation with God. One is that we must repent and confess our sin in order to be forgiven. The other is that we must do everything within our power to *avoid* ever willfully *re-*

peating the sin. Would it follow then that in order to be forgiven for the sins of divorce and remarriage, God would demand that we sin again in another divorce?

Before we get into an application from God's Word on the solution to all of this, let's examine once again the problem as I have sketched it throughout this book thus far.

The Problem Restated

In the Old Testament, Moses allowed divorce because of the hardness of heart in God's chosen people. Jesus Christ changed the ground rules for divorce by transforming the heart of the believer. "Therefore, if anyone is in Christ, he is a new creation; the old has gone, the new has come" (2 Corinthians 5:17). In his answer to the Pharisees, he clearly presented himself as the solution to the divorce question raised in Matthew 19:3–9. Therefore, a Christian who divorces denies Christ's lordship, and anyone who remarries denies his lordship a second time and is obligated to reconcile. Who would argue that such a person is not in deep trouble? While these sins (including the sin of adultery) demand God's just judgment, one may yet hope for a miracle if this tangled mess of scrambled lives were made palatable to God by salting them with an absolute repentance. I am referring to a repentance similar to that made by the children of Israel when they said to God, "Do with us whatever you think best, but please rescue us now" (Judges 10:15). I believe Scripture does give us a way to repent through the application of this very command.

God's Solution for the Remarried Divorcee

A solution must exist, we agree, since the Bible nowhere classified any of the sins under discussion as unforgivable. When we are dealing with the symptom of divorce

114

and the very real problem of remarriage, the difficulty we experience in recognizing any solution from God is our failure to isolate God's exact requirements for forgiveness *after* the remarriage is a fact.

There are two solid biblical examples that will help us focus on God's solution for this remarriage trap, and neither of them involves breaking up the second marriage. In presenting these I ask for two things; first, your indulgence because if a simple answer were available I could quote a verse or two to prove the point; second, your careful consideration of what God may be implying apart from any preconceived conclusions you may already have made. I realize the ease of emotionally prejudging this situation. Each of us has thoughts and conclusions on this matter which have been formulated over many years of Bible study. Yet I plead with you to be open to what God might be saying through these two applications.

Because I was afraid that some readers might inadvertently close their minds to anything out of harmony with their previous conclusions, I asked several of my friends to react to what you are about to read. One was very negative. He claimed that these applications nearly destroyed the argument that had already been built to this point, claiming that I had even contradicted earlier positions. Yet I think that rather than contradicting anything said thus far, these two examples represent the forgiveness that God holds out to each sinner every day. It may appear contradictory at first glance, I admit, but so do a few verses of Scripture—until they are studied and reasoned.

God tells us *not* to sin. Then he tells us that if we *do* sin anyway, there is still forgiveness. Is that contradictory? The apostle John tells us this: "My dear children, I write this to you so that you will not sin. But if anybody does sin, we have one who speaks to the Father in our defense—Jesus Christ the Righteous One" (1 John 2:1).

I have also said in this book, "Do not divorce, and do not remarry"; and now I add, "But if you did anyway, there is still forgiveness and hope!" I do not consider this any more of a contradiction than 1 John 2:1. My applications are based upon the same Defender, Supporter, and Forgiver—Jesus Christ.

One last point: These applications are for remarried divorcees *only,* not the divorcee looking for a loophole so that he or she may remarry! With that stipulation clearly made, my friend with the negative reaction felt very much at ease with both applications as well as the conclusions.

The First Biblical Application

Beginning in Genesis, the Old Testament points sinners to the forgiveness for which we are searching in the person of Jesus Christ. We must begin there also. The first hint of our Savior appears in Genesis 3:15, and by chapter 12 God is at work unfolding his plan of salvation. God promised Abram that he would make of him a great nation (verse 12). By beginning in Genesis we will better understand the application I wish to make—God's solution to today's divorce-remarriage trap—through Abraham's unquestioning obedience.

God promised Abram a son by his wife Sarai (Genesis 15:4), who was already beyond her age of bearing children. God's promise was that Abram's seed would number with the stars of heaven. Now, our Father's promise included Abram's *one and only* wife, the wife of his youth, Sarai. But Abram and Sarai together thought they could "help" God a bit. In their human impatience for the promise to be fulfilled, Sarai sinfully concocted an idea of rushing the whole affair by allowing Abram to use her handmaid, Hagar, to conceive. Abram did, and Hagar conceived—the wrong son, Ishmael. God had to remind Abram that his promise was through Abram's only wife.

God made a covenant with Abram. He changed his name to Abraham and promised Abraham that he would be the "father of many nations" (Genesis 17:4–8). God also changed Sarai's name to Sarah and said she would have a son. Abraham was already ninety-nine years old and fell face down laughing (Genesis 17:17) at God when he heard this. Sarah was ninety years old and she also laughed in disbelief (Genesis 18:12). God told them: "You will call him Isaac. . . . And as for Ishmael, I have heard you. . . . But my covenant I will establish with Isaac, whom Sarah will bear to you by this time next year" (Genesis 17:19–21). God's way proved to be the only means for the fulfillment of his grace.

But Abraham was not beyond God's help even when he doubted. God had to ask, "Is anything too hard for the Lord?" (Genesis 18:14). Isaac *was* born and Abraham became *very* attached to Isaac—a most important point to remember! After Isaac was weaned, God said, "Take your son, your only son Isaac, whom you love, and go to the region of Moriah. Sacrifice him there as a burnt offering" (Genesis 22:2). Abraham's mouth must have fallen open a mile! Was his possessiveness of that child so obvious? Yet he obeyed God, and in doing so he proved to God (and to himself) that he loved God more than Isaac. This too is an important point to bear in mind.

Abraham traveled three long days to the place where he would surrender his only son. He obeyed God in the face of many heart-rending questions from Isaac concerning the source of the offering. Through it all, Abraham held true to his faith, purpose, and duty to obey God. He prepared the altar upon which he would sacrifice Isaac. Isaac watched and asked questions. Finally, Abraham had to explain to Isaac what the Lord had required of him. We read that Abraham "bound his son Isaac and laid him on the altar, on top of the wood." The Bible tells us more: Abraham "reached out his hand

and took the knife to slay his son. But the angel of the Lord called out to him from heaven, 'Abraham! Abraham! . . . Do not lay a hand on the boy. . . . Do not do anything to him. Now I know that you fear God, because you have not withheld from me your son, your only son' " (Genesis 22:9–12).

Abraham had actually reached out and taken the knife into his hand! He *was* willing to obey, both physically and spiritually. He was only a breath away from fulfilling God's command! Thus he demonstrated full trust in the fullness of God's authority in his life in a manner that seemed contrary to *every* human analysis—performing a deed that would have put an earthly end to Isaac, together with the promises God had so clearly made concerning Isaac, those extending to us today. He was *willing* to obey God, even in the face of not understanding! What a drama! What faith! What obedience! Abraham did not have to sacrifice Isaac, but he had to be *willing* to. In other words, Abraham had to literally slay his possessiveness for Isaac, all his hope for his son, all his love for him, in order to see God's divine love for both of them. This is still another important point to remember.

What has all this to do with forgiveness and divorce-remarriage in the twentieth century? At this point, I wish to address the divorced-remarried Christian in a personal way. You are remarried against God's will—for at least the first time. Since you have disobeyed God through divorce and then again through a remarriage, you are now showing a possessiveness for a marital position to which you have no biblical right. He asks any who want forgiveness to deny themselves totally. He even asks that they be *willing* to leave "home or wife or brothers or parents or children for the sake of the kingdom of God" (Luke 18:29). He may now be asking you to give up the possessiveness you have for your second husband or wife, as he asked Abraham to slay his possessiveness of Isaac. I am sure God is demanding this surrender from you before he will forgive you. He said, "If you live according to the sinful nature, you will die; but if by the Spirit you put to death the misdeeds of the body, you will live" (Romans 8:13). Forgiveness (an act of God) follows repentance (an act of man) which requires turning *away* from the sin and turning toward God instead.

I believe God is saying to the truly repentant and penitent Christian caught in this mess, "I am the God of your father, the God of Abraham, the God of Isaac and the God of Jacob" (Exodus 3:6), the same God who told Abraham to sacrifice Isaac! Now he is saying to you, Go to my altar and sacrifice the possession of your second wife (or husband) and the love for her which placed me second. In other words, he is asking, Who means more to you, your present spouse or I?

Would you be willing to *listen and act* if God asked you for a sacrifice such as Abraham's? Would you be willing to obey? Be sure of one thing: he's asking. In fact, he's commanding!

If you are unable to truthfully say you would do *anything* God demanded to regain his complete favor (that is, if you are still holding back, looking for an excuse or a way out of this), then simply disregard the rest of this and continue in your sin. This application is not designed (nor intended) to become just another way of escape. It is based on Scripture which does not allow sinners a way out short of meaningful, sincere, and undefiled repentance. We know what is required for absolute and sincere repentance. You can't neglect that requirement.

If, on the other hand, you are overwrought, torn apart, sincerely sick of this sin, and disgusted with yourself to the point of being willing to do utterly anything the Lord God commanded, then read on, because God asked Abraham to relinquish his *possessiveness* for Isaac in a unique way. He was instructed to offer Isaac as a blood sacrifice upon an altar on top of a mountain.

Now, these days God isn't satisfied with blood rituals; Christ's blood sacrifice was once and for all. Today we are required to become *living sacrifices* instead. Paul says, "I urge you . . . to offer your bodies as living sacrifices, holy and pleasing to God" (Romans 12:1).

Thus the New Testament becomes new and refreshing. God's law no longer demands blood. "For this reason it (God's law) can never, by the same sacrifices repeated endlessly year after year, make perfect those who draw near to worship. If it could, would they not have stopped being offered? . . . it is impossible for the blood of bulls and goats to take away sins. Therefore, when Christ came into the world he said (to his Father in heaven):

> 'Sacrifice and offering you did not desire, but a body you prepared for me; with burnt offerings and sin offerings you were not pleased. Then I said, "Here I am—it is written about me in the scroll—I have come to do your will, O God." '

First [the writer of Hebrews continues] he said, 'Sacrifices and offerings, burnt offerings and sin offerings you did not desire, nor were you pleased with them' (although the law required them to be made). Then he said, 'Here I am, I have come to do your will.' He sets aside the first to establish the second. And by that will, we have been made holy through the sacrifice of the body of Jesus Christ once for all" (Hebrews 10:1–10).

God tells us this also: "You have not come to a mountain that can be touched . . . with fire . . . But you have come to Mount Zion, to the heavenly Jerusalem, the city of the living God. You have come to thousands upon thousands of angels in joyful assembly, to the church of the firstborn, whose names are written in heaven" (Hebrews 12:18–23a).

Yes, you must come to the Church! This is where in the twentieth century *living* sacrifices are made pleasing to God. The New Testament calls God's people "living stones" (1 Peter 2:5) built into a spiritual house (the Church) offering spiritual sacrifices acceptable to God.

God, therefore, may be saying to you: Come to my Church, my spiritual house, Mount Zion, the assembly of the heavenly Jerusalem. Yes, come to my Church as a public deed—a visible fruit of repentance. Prove to my representatives in the Church that your greatest love is for me. Show them an attitude change. Sacrifice your love for your second marriage in utter regret so that I can forgive you. Do it humbly in the presence of those to whom I have given the keys to the kingdom of heaven. Come to Mount Zion and commit your error and sin to me in perfect surrender. Give me 100 percent by turning away from the possessiveness (which marked your second marriage) and your past arrogance (which fed your first sin of divorce) and, instead, turn with confidence wholeheartedly to me. Prove that your stubborn will has been crucified in my Son, Jesus, and that your new relationship to him is that of servant to the Lord, expressed now through public obedience to me and my Word. Confess that divorce and remarriage are no longer a willful part of your desire, no matter what that decision might cost you. Mutually agree to announce to the world that your sin, while defiling both of you, dishonored me and denied the lordship of your Savior, his body (the Church), and the power of the Holy Spirit. Yes, agree to speak out against divorce and remarriage now that you know and understand the sin associated with it.

God asked Abraham to *prove* that he loved God more than Isaac. Isaac was not the problem, nor is your wrongfully acquired mate. The problem is spiritual: a matter of will, pride, and selfishness.

God's Word says, "Water spilled on the ground . . . cannot be recovered. . . . But God does not take away life;

instead, he devises ways so that a banished person may not remain estranged from him" (2 Samuel 14:14). What ways does God devise? Sincere repentance, confession, and his divine forgiveness! Water once spilled on the ground cannot be gathered up again. Instead, we need the miracle of God's forgiveness. But how—under these circumstances?

There is a way, and it brings me to my second biblical example. God did *not* require David to undo his wrongful marriage to Bathsheba. Instead, there was absolute, divine forgiveness.

The Second Biblical Application
No Bible character encompasses the full range of human nature and sin more graphically than David. He is called a man after God's own heart in 1 Samuel 13:14; yet he married Bathsheba, whom he had before defiled and whose husband he had murdered, causing an affront to the ordinance of marriage. David's adultery with Bathsheba, his killing of Uriah, and his marriage to her all displeased God; yet David was not required to divorce her to prove his repentance.

It is interesting to note that the Bible is faithful to tell about the faults of godly men. David's sins are an example, and this account is given for our instruction. When David committed these sins, he had been entrusted with the sword of justice himself. He became, thereby, the object of his own justice and judgment. This point is vividly outlined for us in the encounter David had with the prophet Nathan. Nathan told David a parable that obligated David to condemn himself: " 'There were two men in a certain town, one rich and the other poor. The rich man had a very large number of sheep and cattle, but the poor man had nothing except one little ewe lamb he had bought. He raised it, and it grew up with him and his children. It shared his food, drank from his cup and even slept in his arms. It was like a daughter to him. Now a traveler came to the rich man, but the rich man refrained from taking one of his own sheep or cattle to prepare a meal for the traveler who had come to him. Instead, he took the ewe lamb that belonged to the poor man and prepared it for the one who had come to him.' David burned with anger against the man and said to Nathan, 'As surely as the Lord lives, the man who did this deserves to die! He must pay for that lamb four times over, because he did such a thing and had no pity' " (2 Samuel 12:1–6).

David's sin was adultery with Bathsheba. David had been resting on his bed when he decided to walk out on the roof of the house. Across the street he saw a beautiful woman taking a bath. He lusted, desired, and coveted her. He sent out his messenger to bring her to him. "She came to him and he slept with her" (2 Samuel 11:4). Later she realized that she had conceived a child and told David, "I am pregnant" (2 Samuel 11:5). David tried to cover his sin by ordering her husband Uriah to return from battle (hopefully to sleep with his wife so he would assume he was the father of David's child). When Uriah refused to go into his own house the first night, because of loyalty to comrades, David kept him over another night and made him drunk hoping this would send him off to bed with his wife Bathsheba, but to no avail. David continued to plot a cover-up until he planned and carried out the murder of Uriah by sending him to the front lines of battle to be killed. He accomplished this with a written order given to and carried by the victim himself. When Bathsheba heard of her husband's death, she mourned, and "after the time of mourning was over, David had her brought to his house, and she became his (unjustly acquired) wife" (2 Samuel 11:27).

The reader must be careful not to react to this by thinking that Bathsheba's husband was dead and therefore David and Bathsheba could rightly marry, lest one condone the act of murder to attain one's goal in marriage. The fact stands before us that the adultery, falsehood, murder, and the marriage (referred to as the "case of Uriah the Hittite" in 1 Kings 15:5) was very displeasing to God and contrary to his will and way.

Is this the David of the Bible? Yes, it is! And let every one of us also recognize ourselves here and understand what the best of us are when left to our own selfish desires, sins, and cover-ups.

Nathan summed it all up when he said to David, "By doing this you have made the enemies of the Lord show utter contempt" (2 Samuel 12:14). Think about how David's sin parallels those we are considering. He committed adultery, he wrongfully plotted out the acquisition of another man's wife, and he married her. David knew better, just as the Christian knows in his or her heart before God that he or she is not pleasing God in a civil divorce and second marriage. God had called David a man after his own heart. So we know that David knew better. Did God, therefore, now insist that David rid himself of Bathsheba in order to prove repentance and effect forgiveness? No! God demanded and received total repentance and granted divine forgiveness to David while allowing David to *remain married* to Bathsheba. God even went a step further. He blessed that marriage with a second son, Solomon, and caused that lineage to bring forth our Savior, Jesus Christ!

Read the first verse of the New Testament, "A record of the genealogy of Jesus Christ the son of David..." and the words of the sixth verse of Matthew 1, "David was the father of Solomon, whose mother had been Uriah's wife." Scripture is very honest with us. David was forgiven while being allowed to remain married to a wrongfully acquired wife, but the Bible never forgot whose wife she really was.

David's confession included all the biblical aspects of

true and sincere repentance. Here is part of what David felt and said to God in humble regret: "Have mercy upon me, O God. . . . blot out my transgressions. . . . my sin is ever before me. . . . wash me, and I will be whiter than snow. . . . Hide your face from my sins. . . . create in me a pure heart, O God, and renew a steadfast spirit within me. . . . do not take your Holy Spirit from me. Restore to me the joy of your salvation. . . . You do not delight in sacrifices, or I would bring it; you do not take pleasure in burnt offerings. The sacrifices of God are a broken spirit; a broken and a contrite heart, O God, you will not despise" (Psalm 51).

As God tells us, David *was* forgiven and then blessed in that wrongfully acquired marriage because he had truly repented and feared God; and being convicted of his sin, he confessed it and was freely forgiven.

Therefore, if a Christian has already violated God's institution of marriage twice (by divorcing and remarrying), it would be foolish to insist that he or she commit yet another sin (divorcing a second time) as proof of repentance. If we require this, we are forgetting David and God's dealings with him. God wants an uncompromised broken spirit, *your* broken and contrite heart, as evidence of your living sacrifice.

Again, those who demand leaving the second marriage assume that such a deed of sacrifice will secure forgiveness. But we are never forgiven by doing penance. Paul states, "He saved us, not because of righteous things we had done, but because of his mercy. He saved us through the washing of rebirth and renewal by the Holy Spirit" (Titus 3:5).

Remember the words of Psalm 51: "The sacrifices of God are a broken spirit; a broken and contrite heart, O God, you will not despise." The entire solution to the divorce-remarriage trap is sincere repentance followed by divine forgiveness. God is sovereign even in those situations we consider to be hopeless.

A Necessary Warning

To the divorced but not yet remarried reader who has now caught a glimpse of God's forgiving nature for those already divorced and remarried—beware! None of what is written in Scripture concerning forgiveness of sin should ever be used in the plotting of a sin. Such thinking and planning is an abomination before the Lord. None of the material in this chapter can be considered by a divorcee (not yet remarried) as a guideline condoning remarriage. God promises to forgive, but his promise is never a license to sin.

Though it is true that after sincere repentance we will receive grace equal to the sin, it is also true that those who are redeemed are to be *dead* to sin. If we are dead to sin, we aren't preplanning it! If we plan a sin in advance, we are servants to the devil and the devil is our master. Jesus said, "No one can serve two masters. Either he will hate the one and love the other, or he will be devoted to the one and despise the other" (Matthew 6:24). Either we serve the devil or Christ. We cannot serve both, and a preplanned sin is a futile effort to serve both. Again, God's promise of grace for the sinner is never license to sin.

To the remarried divorcee, let me say that God promised that he would deal mercifully with you and cause his Holy Spirit to soften your heart completely if you ask him. "The Lord is not slow in keeping his promises, as some understand slowness. He is patient with you, not wanting anyone to perish, but everyone to come to repentance" (2 Peter 3:9).

If you are sorry that you have offended God in your sin, but still *feel* hopelessly lost in the consequence (adultery) of the remarriage, then remember the words of God: " 'Come now, let us reason together,' says the Lord, 'though your sins are like scarlet, they shall be as white as snow, though they are red as crimson, they shall be like wool' " (Isaiah 1:18). "Repent, then, and turn to God, so that your sins may be wiped out" (Acts 3:19). Note, God didn't say "overlooked" when referring to your sins; he said "wiped out!" "For if we confess our sins, he is faithful and just and will forgive our sins and purify us from all unrighteousness" (1 John 1:9). Note that God didn't say he would allow you to live in the consequential adultery; he said he would *purify* from *all* unrighteousness! "If anybody does sin, we have one who speaks to the Father in our defense—Jesus Christ, the Righteous One. He is the atoning sacrifice for our sins, and not only for ours but also for the sins of the whole world" (1 John 2:1, 2). Note that he said Christ's sacrifice was for the sins of the whole world. How could any sinner amass so great a debt as to bankrupt that potential? God has an indisputable record of forgiving and forgetting.

You may only be one in a million to come before the church elders to confess your sin, but that is the ratio with which God seems to work. Look at Israel. There was only a remnant there also. In the New Testament God again says, "Many are invited, but few are chosen" (Matthew 22:14). Be sure of one thing: "That he who began a good work in you will carry it on to completion until the day of Christ Jesus" (Philippians 1:6). What a Savior!

TEN
A Perspective

Regardless of the predicament in which we find ourselves, if we are able to come back to Christ penitently (knowing that his blood was shed to rid us of all our dark blots, conflicts, doubts, fightings, and fears), it's only because the Lamb of God has pardoned, cleansed, and relieved us from our sin as he promised he would. But something occurs before all this. The Holy Spirit is at work first. David didn't come to God with his sin; God came to David through the prophet Nathan's confrontation. But God's Spirit was also at work in David's heart to allow David to *see* the sin of murder and the wrongful acquisition of another man's wife. When David realized his sin, he did what all of us must do: he confessed it. Then he received pardon.

Part of David's prayer was, "Take not thy holy spirit from me' (Psalm 51:11b, KJV), and the Holy Spirit was *not* taken from David. Nor does God take his Spirit from us when we seek forgiveness. The Holy Spirit was probably already at work in your heart long before you arrived at this point of your life. It should now be obvious to you that the core problem you had in marriage or divorce was a spiritual one. Therefore, I would be remiss if I didn't touch on the electrifying power of the Holy Spirit that not only convicts us of our sin, but pulls us back to Christ's dynamic forgiveness, love, and tender mercy.

God is able to make a believing couple acceptable and worthy, as he did with David and Bathsheba, if he is given full control and undivided management of those redeemed and forgiven lives. In order for this to happen, Christ's Holy Spirit must dwell fully in the heart of the forgiven sinner. All of us must give our Savior his rightful place as Lord and Master of our entire lives. If we hold back (and try to manage our own lives through the exercise of our free will), we will remain worldly and carnal while heading for certain failure. Paul warns us against this danger, taking important note of the fact that we remain Christians even while doing things backwards. He calls us brothers: "Brothers, I could not address you as spiritual but as worldly" (1 Corinthians 3:1), indicating the danger of those senseless spiritual problems into which all of us as believers fall from time to time. The point that God would have us understand here is this: Don't wait for another marital *breakdown* to force the ultimate spiritual *breakthrough.*

If only we would listen to God! Think of the exciting spiritual growth we would experience if we would only avoid deliberate disregard of his leadings. To experience spiritual leading and growth requires paying attention to God, giving him management of day-by-day problems, and maintaining his fullness hour by hour. The question is, "How can this be accomplished?" There are no mystical answers to becoming filled with the Holy Spirit, although there are some simple steps which each of us must be reminded to take from time to time.

The first step in becoming controlled by the Holy Spirit is to recognize that he is already in your heart! The Holy Spirit is in the heart of every believer, even though some ignore him. When you asked Jesus into your heart

130

at conversion, you received the Holy Spirit also. Paul assures every Christian of this fact: "If anyone does not have the Spirit of Christ, he does not belong to Christ" (Romans 8:9). Before conversion, the Holy Spirit was also at work within you, in a different way, pointing you to Christ. Further evidence of the Spirit's presence in your heart was displayed all those times you prayed about your divorce and remarriage. Each time we pray, the Holy Spirit prompts us to pray. The Holy Spirit is the One who focuses guilt upon each sin and then calls us to repentance and confession.

Don't you think it is safe to assume that the real problem you had (the spiritual problem) was partly caused by your grieving the Holy Spirit and quenching his input? Don't you agree that this is perhaps the reason you began showing the symptoms of this problem in your marital relationship which ended in divorce? It's the same with all of us when we grieve and quench the Holy Spirit. But even though you persisted in grieving him, you may still take comfort in knowing that *grieving* and *quenching* the Spirit are forgivable and reconcilable.

None of us should think for a moment that we are unique if we've experienced disturbing spiritual problems. All Christians at times react to situations in an unscriptural way instead of allowing God's Spirit to help them. All of us have experienced emptiness, depression, and periods when we've turned from God's way. No believer is exempt from this; rather, we have all fallen and sinned, and every one of us needs to be constantly filled and refilled with the Holy Spirit. This is nothing new, and you are not the first or last person to require forgiveness. You are not the first to need a recharge of the Holy Spirit—the power that comes with being filled. That is necessary for each of us when we have allowed ourselves to suffer the disillusionment of doing whatever we want to do just because it feels good at the moment. We've all done that, so join the rest of us sinners (including David) who are now forgiven and whole again.

The second step in becoming filled with the Holy Spirit is prayerfully *asking* him to become Lord, King, and Master of your life. Pledge to relinquish yourself to him completely, including every juncture of your life, every decision, hope, and problem. Being in tune with his Holy Spirit gives us a new and exciting insight into what God has prepared for us. When we are truly walking in his Spirit, we have answers from his Word within us.

Third, before Jesus becomes the Lord of your life, you must first confess all known sins (even as David had to do) and obey the instruction of Ephesians 5:18: "Be filled with the Spirit." You cannot become spiritually whole if you seek only forgiveness and disregard the necessity of being filled with the Holy Spirit.

This fact is illustrated in what I see every day as a dentist. A patient may come in with decayed teeth. Some decay is clearly visible while other areas require X-rays to discover them. It's the same with sinning. Some sins are obvious, while others require God's X-rays to make them known to us. In dentistry, we remove the decay from the tooth, but this is only half the procedure required to restore the tooth. If we'd stop (and many wish we would) after the decay is properly removed, the tooth (even with its clean cavity) would decay further and faster than before. That's why we fill them! It is not unlike that with forgiveness. Forgiveness is only the first step. After our hearts are cleansed from sin, we must be protected by the filling of the Holy Spirit to prevent further decay.

God will repair broken lives, but they must first be made clean so that the Spirit's indwelling can have a mending effect. Once you are clean and have the Spirit's filling, you will no longer seek to satisfy the old evil desires that led to the first defeat—divorce—or the second surrender—a remarriage. Paul assures us of this when he says, "Live by the Spirit, and you will not gratify the desires of your sinful nature. . . . The acts of the sinful nature are obvious: sexual immorality, impurity and debauchery; idolatry and witchcraft; hatred, discord, jealousy, fits of rage, selfish ambition, dissensions, factions and envy; drunkenness, orgies, and the like. . . . But the fruit of the Spirit is love, joy, peace, patience, kindness, goodness, faithfulness, gentleness, and self-control. . . . Since we (now) live by the Spirit, let us keep in step with the Spirit" (Galatians 5:16–25).

The fourth step is to stop reacting to problems that only Christ can solve. When we insist on reacting to our problems, we usually end up bungling them even more, which only forces us into the next mistake—rationalizing away the first mistake. David knew well the judgment he deserved. Death! But because David repented, God said: "You are not going to die" (2 Samuel 12:13). David didn't rationalize his sin; instead he confessed it openly before God and man. Since it is recorded in holy Scripture, he also confesses it to us.

It is through repentance and confession that we can be filled with and walk in the Holy Spirit. Christ exchanges penalty places with us, and this switch solves the problem, eliminates the symptom, and diffuses the effects. This is how we can live righteous lives while yet being imperfect. He is our atoning sacrifice (or substitution) for the perfection that God requires and for the sinlessness we are unable to deliver.

No one is able to earn salvation through obedience. No one can earn God's forgiveness, since Christ has already paid the total debt. "For he has rescued us from the dominion of darkness and brought us into the kingdom of the Son he loves, in whom we have redemption, the forgiveness of sins" (Colossians 1:13, 14).

Salvation *is* forgiveness. Remember the sacrifice Abraham was asked to make? There are many parallels between Abraham's story and the final once-for-all sacrifice Jesus Christ made for sinners. Neither salvation nor forgiveness is ever merited, and neither is attained by penance. Both come as a free gift from God through the Holy Spirit.

The fifth step is to *ask* God to fill you with the Holy Spirit. He will! He commanded us to be filled in Ephesians 5:18, and he does not tell us to do things outside of his will; therefore, he will accomplish it. Jesus said, "If you then, though you are evil, know how to give good gifts to your children, how much more will your Father in heaven give the Holy Spirit to those who ask him" (Luke 11:13).

Of course this request must be sincerely made and coupled to a full confession of all sins. The filling will be instantaneous because God said it would be, and we are to take him at his word. The fact that we have received the command to be filled is proof that it will happen when we ask. Believing this makes the next step even easier.

Sixth, thank him. Thank him in the same breath you asked him. Prove your faith by thanking him immediately for what he has guaranteed he would do and therefore did. Believe it whether you feel differently or not. God works with facts, not feelings. He said he would fill you; therefore, he *has* filled you. If you feel nothing, there may be good reason. Perhaps this is only the first time you fully surrendered your life to Jesus Christ as Lord and Master. As he now grows within you, your capacity will increase so that each filling, while just as full, will be greater than before. It will be more noticeable too. This is why feelings are not as important as simply believing.

After the filling, you must learn to walk in the Spirit. Becoming filled and being able to walk in the Spirit is the tremendously exciting state of living without the penalty of sin while still sometimes sinning. Confusing? Not really. You will sin, but each sin is forgiven when confessed; therefore, the bottom line with the Father in heaven is the perfection earned by Jesus Christ on your behalf. He became sin so that you might become the righteousness of God! Ponder that for a moment. "God made him (Jesus) who had no sin to be sin for us, so that in him we might become the righteousness of God" (2 Corinthians 5:21). God the Father did this, not so that you won't sin anymore, but because you *will* sin again. The good news is that your sins have been, are, and will be completely forgiven only because of the exchange Jesus Christ willfully and joyfully made with you, for you, and because he loves you.

With the knowledge that Jesus Christ bought and paid for you, he wants you to now live in the joy of your salvation—being filled with his Holy Spirit. Is it too much to ask, considering he wants you to benefit from his *gift* to you? "Be filled with the Holy Spirit," he commands you—for your own good, not his! This is his gift of grace, meaning that he will accept you in spite of your unacceptable condition. Christ's sacrifice is nearly incomprehensible in its effects and benefits for you. How it must grieve him when you shun his own Holy Spirit poured out for your joy!

Not living with the fullness of the Holy Spirit causes anything but joy; in fact, it causes conflicts, according to God's Word. Paul said, "In my inner being I delight in God's law; but I see another law at work in the members of my body, waging war against the law of my mind and making me a prisoner of the law of sin at work within my members. What a wretched man I am! Who will rescue me from this body of death? Thanks be to God—through Jesus Christ our Lord" (Romans 7:22–25).

No doubt the most beautiful aspect of the Spirit's indwelling is his mending effect. Men go to the world to find hope and peace, but what is their reward? Disillusionment! Jesus said, "My peace I give you. I do not give to you as the world gives" (John 14:27). The solution is never found in the world or its courts. It is found in Jesus Christ's faithfulness, for "we know that in all things God works for the good of those who love him, who have been called according to his purpose" (Romans 8:28). His purpose is to work out *his* plan for your life through the direction and guidance of his Holy Spirit. His plan does not include divorce, since from the beginning it was not so. Are you now able to testify that the love of Christ and his plan for your life constrains you and compels you to never consider the sin of divorce again? Would you like to be sure that you will maintain this conviction the rest of your life? Then follow a simple suggestion.

Set aside time each day for your own personal devotions, and make this time the highest priority and most important part of your day. Keep it uninterruptible. Early morning is a good time for this. Speak to God in prayer, but *also* let him speak to you—through his Word. This beautiful exchange can never be overestimated! After beginning a day in close communion with God, your entire outlook will change because you are off on the right foot under his power, influence, and guidance; but best of all, you are under his protection and love. This is how the fullness of the Holy Spirit is best maintained, thereby guaranteeing you a continuing and meaningful indwelling which will produce further spiritual blessings.

Every Christian must admit that except for God's undeserved grace and kindness toward us, every last one of us would have had to suffer the same torment of marital distress that each divorced person has had to endure in his or her sinning, and each of us would have had to learn this lesson the hard way.

We might yet find ourselves suffering through hardships such as a marital storm if we don't diligently maintain a rigorous Bible study of our own and the constant filling of his Holy Spirit. With this important perspective in focus we can and will remain happily married until death parts us. The love we have for our partners is a gift from God. This is what makes it so precious, enduring, and endearing to him and to us.

Let us thank God for his gift of love and pray for its ever deepening growth. Families are important to God! He considers us a part of his family. He as Father, Jesus as our bridegroom, and we as the bride of Christ are all welded together in a permanent bond of marriage through the power of his Holy Spirit for eternity. God hates divorce and has promised never to divorce us; rather, he will forgive us, accept us without any merit, and grant us eternal reconciliation with him. Praise his fantastic name!